PONZIMONIUM

HOW SCAM ARTISTS ARE RIPPING OFF AMERICA

U.S. COMMODITY FUTURES TRADING COMMISSION (CFTS)

Skyhorse Publishing

Skyhorse Publishing books may be purchased in bulk at special discounts for sales promotion, corporate gifts, fund-raising, or educational purposes. Special editions can also be created to specifications. For details, contact the Special Sales Department, Skyhorse Publishing, 307 West 36th Street, 11th Floor, New York, NY 10018 or info@skyhorsepublishing.com.

Skyhorse® and Skyhorse Publishing® are registered trademarks of Skyhorse Publishing, Inc.®, a Delaware corporation.

Visit our website at www.skyhorsepublishing.com.

10 9 8 7 6 5 4 3 2 1

Library of Congress Cataloging-in-Publication Data is available on file.

Cover design by Rain Saukas

ISBN: 978-1-5107-0788-7
Ebook ISBN: 978-1-5107-0792-4

Printed in the United States of America

Contents

About the US Commodity Futures Trading Commission (CFTC)

Congress created the US Commodity Futures Trading Commission in 1974 as an independent agency with the mandate to regulate commodity futures and option markets in the United States. The CFTC's fellow federal financial regulatory agencies include the Securities and Exchange Commission (SEC), the *Federal Deposit Insurance Corporation (FDIC)*, the *Federal Reserve Board*, and the Office of the Comptroller of the Currency (OCC). The CFTC's mandate has been renewed and expanded several times since 1974, most recently with the Dodd-Frank Wall Street Reform and Consumer Protection Act, signed into law by President Barack Obama on July 21, 2010. Dodd-Frank ushers in a new era for the CFTC by expanding its regulatory authority to the over-the-counter derivatives markets. Over-the-counter derivatives previously have not been regulated in the United States and were at the center of the 2008 financial crisis.

FDIC—*Federal agency that regulates national banks*
FEDERAL RESERVE BOARD—*Federal agency that regulates certain state banks, bank holding companies, and foreign bank activity in the United States*

In 1974, the majority of futures trading took place in the agricultural sector. The CFTC's history demonstrates, among other things, how the futures industry has become increasingly varied over time and encompasses a vast array of complex financial futures contracts.

Today, the CFTC assures the economic utility of the futures markets by encouraging their competitiveness and efficiency, protecting market participants against fraud, manipulation, and abusive trading practices, and by ensuring the financial integrity of the clearing process. Through effective oversight, the CFTC enables the futures markets to serve the important function of providing a means for price discovery and offsetting price risk.

The CFTC's mission is to protect market users and the public from fraud, manipulation, and abusive practices related to the sale of commodity and financial futures and options—and now, over-the-counter derivatives—and to foster open, competitive, and financially sound futures and option markets.

The CFTC relies on the public as an important source of information in carrying out its regulatory and enforcement responsibilities. Under a new provision in the Dodd-Frank Act, whistle-blowers may be awarded monetarily by the CFTC for original information that leads to the successful enforcement of a CFTC action. This provision will make it easier for whistle-blowers to come forward with relevant information, helping to prosecute more scam artists and thus saving American taxpayers and consumers money in the long run. You may contact the CFTC to report suspicious activities or transactions that may involve the trading of commodity futures contracts or commodity options, including those that involve foreign currency. The CFTC may be contacted through its toll-free telephone number, 1-866-FON-CFTC (1-866-366-2382), via email at enforcement@cftc.gov, or by submitting an online form available through www.cftc.gov/ConsumerProtection. The Commission may use this information in its investigations or enforcement actions, but it does not act on your behalf or represent you in any way.

The CFTC also offers a reparations program that provides an inexpensive, impartial, and efficient forum for customer complaints against futures industry professionals. Customers may bring complaints against futures industry professionals currently or formerly registered with the CFTC if such individuals or firms allegedly violated the antifraud or other provisions of the Commodity Exchange Act. Reparations cases are decided by Judgment Officers or Administrative Law Judges, depending on the size of the claim. For more information, please contact the Office of Proceedings at 202-418-5350 or via email at questions@cftc.gov. Additional information is available online at www.cftc.gov/ConsumerProtection.

Foreword

Every single day, someone somewhere makes a gigantic mistake by giving his or her money to a fraudster. I'm not referring to those "suckers born every minute" types. I'm talking about regular, hardworking folks who play by the rules and think they are making sound investment decisions, often with significant sums of their non-disposable cash. Smooth talking masters of illusion are out there, twisting and turning their stories to convince would-be investors to hand over their funds. The consequences for these "investors" turned victims can be horrific: people losing money for their kids' college funds; for detrimental health care expenses; or for their own retirement. Some lose their entire life savings. Others unknowingly bring friends and family into the scam thinking they are doing them a favor.

A lot of times, fraudsters remain off the radar and get away with their swindles for years and even decades. Many individual investors don't discover the fraud until they are faced with an economic downturn or some time-sensitive need. Then, when they try to retrieve their investments, they are told, "Nope, you can't have your money back right now." That's when they discover that they have given their money to a fraudster. The funds were all part of a scam and the money is simply gone—kaput.

What the fraudsters do in that time is even more amazing. You should see the stuff crooks do with other people's money.

Fortunately, these con artists are being apprehended and prosecuted. Federal, state, and local law enforcement officials have reported enormous increases in tips and criminal activity since the economic downturn began in 2008. As the markets began to flounder, people wanted out of their investments. However, cash redemptions are dangerous for Ponzi schemes, because when the money runs out, folks start talking. At any one time, enforcement staff at the US Commodity Futures Trading Commission (CFTC) are investigating anywhere between 750 and 1,000 individuals and entities for various violations of the law. Increases in tips and fraud cases also have occurred at the *US Securities and Exchange Commission (SEC)*, at the *Federal Bureau of Investigation (FBI)*, in the states, and in various localities around the world.

The stories you are about to read are actual CFTC cases stemming from investigations that began with the economic downturn. These are real cases with, unfortunately, very real victims. The information is pulled directly from the public case files and

SEC—*Federal agency that regulates securities and securities markets*
FBI—*Federal agency that investigates violations of federal criminal law*

the media; the only added color is in the presentation and the benefit of hindsight. I've changed some names in order to ensure that no one is revictimized by their willingness to come forward and be a part of these cases. There is no shame in being a victim— it could have been, and might well be, any one of us. You'll see that a majority of the defendants in these cases are now in prison or awaiting sentencing.

I've worked in public service for over a quarter of a century and have found that one of the most important things that can be done is to make government less puzzling and perplexing, less mysterious, and yes, less bureaucratic. While there has not been a monumental change in how people see their government over the years, I continue to try and do my part by communicating in a way that lets folks "in" on what is going on. This writing is an effort to continue that work. I hope it will be a satisfying read, but more importantly, that it will help people avoid the tremendous tragedy that so many of our fellow citizens have endured.

Introduction

In December of 2008, the world learned that legendary investment guru Bernard Madoff made off with an estimated $50 billion in what was called the "Mother of all Ponzi Schemes." Ponzi schemes, named after Charles Ponzi, are scams in which early "investors" are given supposed returns paid through funds provided by later investors. Typically, an investment is made and then some "profits" are paid out, prompting the investor to assume that his or her money has increased in value. In actuality, the perpetrators of these schemes—Ponzi, Madoff, or the others described in this book—take the money for themselves. The legal term for this kind of taking is *"misappropriation."* As new investors enter the fraud, supposed returns are offered continually to initial investors, and many times are accompanied by fake account statements. This continues until new money stops flowing in and the investors want their money back. During the 2008 economic downturn, people needed their money back at the same time that there were no new investors. Many "house of cards" scams have fallen and the perpetrators of the swindles have been caught. Charles Ponzi ran these types of scams in the United States until he was deported to Italy, his birthplace, in 1934 as an *"undesirable alien."*

MISAPPROPRIATION—*Taking as one's own entrusted property that is owned by someone else*
UNDESIRABLE ALIEN—*A non-citizen subject to deportation*

Many think that one would have to be foolish to invest in such a scam, but Madoff and other such folks are good at their craft. They often put on a great false front, even fooling the master of illusion, movie director Steven Spielberg. But Spielberg wasn't alone. Even banks, of which we assume would undertake due diligence before funds were invested, got caught in Madoff's web. Investors included Austrian, British, Dutch, Swiss, French, Italian, Portuguese, and Spanish banks. Larry King and the owner of the New York Mets, Fred Wilpon, were duped, as was former LA Dodgers pitcher, Sandy Koufax. Actors Kevin Bacon, Kyra Sedgwick, John Malkovich, and Zsa Zsa Gabor, as well as New York University and New York Law School, a union's health care fund, several trusts, endowments, and nonprofits such as the Elie Wiesel Foundation for Humanity made the widely publicized victims list. Even the International Olympic Committee wasn't immune from the Madoff scam.

While this may have been the largest swindle ever, scores and scores of Ponzis of all sizes and values continue to be unearthed. There have never been more of these scams, and they are occurring all over the world. That's why this publication is called *Ponzimonium*. The cases described here are just as damaging to the victims as was the Madoff scam, and many of them are every bit as complicated and seemingly authentic.

Meanwhile, Madoff traded his Manhattan penthouse for a jail cell for the next 150 years, but the damage he did to those he took advantage of cannot be repaired. Their story and others provide an instructive window into how these schemes operate and how to avoid becoming a Ponzi scheme victim.

To the victims, words cannot express our sorrow at your loss. Let this be a lesson to us all. White-collar crime is a cancer on this nation's soul and our tolerance of it speaks volumes about where we need to go as a nation if we are to survive the current economic troubles we find ourselves facing; because these troubles were of our own making and due solely to unchecked, unregulated greed. We get the government and the regulators that we deserve, so let us be sure to hold not only our government and our regulators accountable, but also ourselves for permitting these situations to occur.

—Harry Markopolos, CFA, CFE a/k/a the Madoff Whistle-blower[1]

ONE

No Client will Ever Lose a Penny

Beau Diamond and Diamond Ventures LLC

"[D]efendant has proven himself a dishonest and untrustworthy person, as evidenced by the crime itself and the fact that he was hiding out from law enforcement when he was arrested. . . . I am not left with a secure feeling about Defendant's release in light of the nature of the allegations, the extent of the monies fraudulently procured by the Defendant, and the potential punishment in the case."

—Thomas B. McCoun III, United States Magistrate Judge[1]

On January 22, 2009, Beau Diamond, the thirty-one-year-old owner and manager of Diamond Ventures LLC, a small company created to trade *off-exchange foreign currency contracts* (forex), sent his investors an email notifying them that "the funds have been lost." He urged them not to "initiate a federal

OFF-EXCHANGE FOREIGN CURRENCY CONTRACTS—
Trading based on changing values of currencies with a commodity or other intermediary outside of an organized exchange

investigation," because if there is a federal investigation, "no one will ever see a penny, and I most likely will be behind bars."[2] When Diamond's investors received his email they were shocked to learn that their investments were gone, because up until that time, Diamond had guaranteed their principal investment and a monthly return.[3] Diamond always told his investors that the maximum loss his fund could sustain was 15 percent, and that he created a reserve account to cover the maximum loss.[4] Indeed, Diamond Ventures' promotional materials stated that the reserve account money "just sits there, unused, untouched and ready to cover this 15 percent maximum loss" and therefore, "no client loses a single penny."[5] What went so drastically wrong that 200 people now faced the total loss of their investments?

For starters, Diamond Ventures never had a reserve account to cover trading losses. Beau Diamond was able to enter into written contracts with his customers guaranteeing them monthly returns of between 2.75 and 5 percent, as well as commission incentives to bring in additional customers because customers were paid from other customers' money.[6] On September 3, 2009, immediately

CLIENTS	GUARANTEED RETURNS	APPROX. INVESTOR DEPOSITS
200	2.75-5% MONTHLY	$37,744,000

following his arrest by federal authorities, the Commodity Futures Trading Commission filed a *civil complaint* charging Diamond and Diamond Ventures with misappropriation and fraud in operating a forex ponzi scheme.

CIVIL COMPLAINT—*Legal document filed by wronged party to start a lawsuit against a wrongdoer*

On December 17, 2009, the United States Attorney's Office for the Middle District of Florida, Tampa Division, filed an eighteen-count indictment against Beau Diamond, charging him with seven counts of *wire fraud*, three counts of *mail fraud*, seven counts of illegal money transactions, and one count of transportation of stolen property. According to the indictment, Diamond collected approximately $37,744,000 from his unsuspecting victims, spending and ultimately losing less than half of that—$15,231,000—on forex trading. Another $15,177,000 was paid back to investors as phantom profits to keep the scheme afloat. The remaining $7,336,000 went to Diamond and his companies for a waterfront condo, a 2006 Lamborghini Gallardo, extended gambling trips to Las Vegas, jewelry, a high-end rental home in Newport Beach, California, as well as vacations to Brazil, the Cayman Islands, and Costa Rica.[7]

Diamond talked a good game and his background made it easy for him to get his foot in the door with many investors.

LOST IN FOREX TRADING	PHANTOM PROFITS	POCKETED BY DIAMOND
$15,231,000	$15,177,000	$7,336,000

> **WIRE FRAUD**—*Criminal fraud committed through use of electronic communications*
> **MAIL FRAUD**—*Criminal fraud committed through use of the mail*

Diamond's parents, Harvey and Marilyn Diamond, were "pillars in the community" and the authors of the popular natural diet and health book series *Fit for Life*.[8] Their connections, and the fact that Harvey Diamond was listed on the incorporation documents for Diamond Ventures, equaled instant affinity to several Sarasota, Florida, investors who were involved in the local natural healing community that followed the *Fit for Life* philosophy.[9] Diamond also had a philosophy that he put into print: a forex book/trading course that he and his employees touted as having "sold very well to traders in over fifty countries."[10, 11]

The Wights*, an average dual-income Sarasota couple nearing retirement, first learned about Diamond Ventures during a dinner held by a vegetarian group at a local restaurant. A couple at their table was talking about their investment with Diamond Ventures and the Diamond family connection. Jane Wight knew of the Diamond family through her involvement with the natural healing community and had been invited to the dinner by an acquaintance of Harvey Diamond. Not long after the dinner, Mrs. Wight's hairdresser, who also was involved in the natural healing community, mentioned her ex-husband was making lots of money with Diamond Ventures. Thereafter, Mrs. Wight contacted the couple who had first told her about Diamond Ventures and learned

---

* Names have been changed to protect the privacy of the individuals.

more about how their investments were doing before contacting Diamond's assistant directly. Mrs. Wight was candid with the Diamond's assistant about their financial situation: the Wights had money set aside for their special-needs adult daughter and thought that Diamond Ventures would be a great opportunity to invest that money and ensure her financial future.[12]

Diamond's assistant sent Mrs. Wight an email describing Diamond Ventures in greater detail and sent copies of the Diamond Ventures contract and earning guarantee schedules. Thereafter, Mrs. Wight and her husband began liquidating some of the investment accounts set aside for their daughter and tapped into their home equity to invest with Diamond Ventures. The information they received indicated that by allowing the earnings on their deposit to compound, they would receive a yearly return of close to 43 percent and that the principal and monthly returns would be "fully guaranteed by a legal contract." Their friends were making money and Beau Diamond represented that "no client loses a single penny," so the Wights made their first deposit.[13]

Over time, prompted by Beau Diamond's solicitations for additional funds with guaranteed bonuses, the Wights invested $200,000 with Diamond Ventures. The Wights made it very clear to Diamond's assistant that they were tapping into the remainder of their home equity loan, liquidating monies set aside for their daughter's care, and using Mr. Wight's IRA account in order to fund additional investments with Diamond Ventures. Diamond's assistant assured the Wights that the "bonuses" were guaranteed as long as the money was left compounding for six months. Unfortunately, after six months, the Wights learned that their entire life savings was gone.[14]

Some investors received the "Diamond Ventures Teleseminar Transcript," thirteen pages of frequently asked questions and answers explaining the world of forex. This document explained that Diamond Ventures operates as an "investment club" limited to "close friends and associates and just strictly through word of mouth" to generate consistent profits while ensuring that "no client ever loses a single penny."[15] Diamond's loquaciousness and diatribe against traders and trading systems not associated with Diamond Ventures reached a noteworthy peak when Diamond stated:

> *This is an interesting fact here. Did you know that literally over 95 percent of all traders never consistently make a profit?*[16]

This should have been a red flag, but as the victims of this fraud eventually discovered, Beau Diamond financed his international vacations, expensive cars, and gambling junkets not by successful forex trading but by using their money to pay for his luxurious lifestyle.[17]

Diamond was put in custody in September 2009 and was twice denied bail due to the severity of the charges against him and the fact that he was a flight risk. After an eight-day jury trial beginning on July 12, 2010, Diamond was found guilty on all eighteen charges.[18] On December 22, 2010, a federal district court judge for the Middle District of Florida sentenced Diamond to 186 months (15½ years) imprisonment on counts one through ten (concurrently) and 120 months imprisonment on counts eleven through eighteen (concurrently), 36 months of supervised release and *restitution* to defrauded investors in the amount of $23,065,090.[19]

RESTITUTION—Money paid by wrongdoer based on loss to wronged party

On December 30, 2010, the United States District Court for the Middle District of Florida entered a final judgment order of restitution and *civil monetary penalty* against Diamond and Diamond Ventures in the CFTC's civil fraud case. In the CFTC's order, the court found that Diamond and Diamond Venture's violations of the antifraud provisions of the Commodity Exchange Act merited an award of restitution in the amount of $1,071,035, plus post-judgment interest, and a civil monetary penalty (CMP) of $3,213,105, plus post-judgment interest. The court found defendants jointly and severally liable for payment of the restitution and CMP amounts.[20]

CIVIL MONETARY PENALTY—Civil fine for violating Commodity Exchange Act or CFTC's rules

Diamond's parents couldn't help him out or his victims. As Diamond told his club members, "My father was essentially whiped [sic] out by this along with many other club members, and my mother lives month to month from a small income that she makes with her husband."[21] In the end, the Diamond Ventures investors can hope that Beau Diamond was prescient when he composed his January 2009 email to them and that he does, in fact, stay "behind bars" for many years to come.

TWO

A Friend to Fraud

Billion Coupons, Inc. and Marvin R. Cooper

"So in that vein, I think your moving (may be for a different reason than I thought) to Panama is a great move. Allows you to resume the OPM [Other People's Money] business without nasty headaches from those bastards from Wall Street and their cronies. All investor/saver [sic] do is transfer the money out of USA into bank accounts in Panama (or any bank outside of USA) then again transfer that money to your trading account. Easy as 1, 2, 3."

—Excerpt from an email to Marvin R. Cooper commenting on his proposed move to Panama in order to avoid being caught[1]

Affinity frauds exploit the trust and camaraderie that exist in groups of people who share a common unifying trait such as ethnicity, religion, age, or in the case of Marvin R. Cooper, deafness. The people who promote affinity scams frequently are—or pretend to be—members of the targeted group, and Cooper was no exception: Marvin R. Cooper is deaf.[2]

Many affinity frauds operate as Ponzi schemes, where new investor money is used to make payments to earlier investors, giving the false illusion of success. Affinity frauds also may operate as pyramid schemes enlisting members of the target group to spread the word about the success of the investment, create an appearance of legitimacy, and bring in new customers. Many times those insiders become unwitting victims of the fraudster's ruse. Billion Coupons was both a pyramid scheme and a Ponzi scheme: investors were organized as "investor groups" with Billion Coupons representatives heading each group and adhering to a commission-based compensation structure based on referrals.[3] In affinity frauds like Billion Coupons, red flags are camouflaged by the common ground that forms the basis of trust and friendship in the group.

Marvin R. Cooper was the CEO, owner, and sole trader of Billion Coupons Inc., a "private investing corporation" in Honolulu, Hawaii.[4] Starting around September of 2007, Cooper began soliciting the deaf communities in the United States and Japan to invest in foreign currency futures contracts with promised returns of 15 to 25 percent a month with little risk.[5] Cooper solicited customers from the deaf community personally and through Billion Coupons representatives, who boasted to potential investors that they were receiving checks every month from their own investments.[6] Cooper and the Billion Coupons representatives proclaimed that the investment opportunity was not open to public investors "as required by federal law," and that Billion Coupons' membership would be limited to United States investors in the United States and ninety-nine investors in Japan before the door closed.[7] In fact, at a March 2008 seminar in Salt Lake City, a Billion Coupons representative warned that there were only six slots remaining: Billion Coupons was going to become a "private hedge fund group."[8]

Cooper touted a "very special" contact network in forex trading that allowed him to use a "high-yield investment plan." A Billion Coupons representative told a prospective customer that Billion Coupons needed more investors because larger funds meant a better investment strategy and higher returns. Though he was making $30,000 to $300,000 each day trading forex and openly discussed his private self-piloted plane and his second home (a multimillion dollar beach-front house in Hawaii), Cooper

RED FLAGS IN THIS SCHEME:

- Promised profits of "15 to 25 percent a month" and claims that more money will bring higher returns—(i.e., you will make lots of money quickly, but it takes more of your money to make money);
- A "private investing corporation" with limited membership—(i.e., exclusivity provides a special bond—this opportunity isn't for everyone: you're special);
- Only six slots left before Billion Coupons becomes a "private hedge fund group" and is closed to the public forever—(i.e., this is a once-in-a-lifetime opportunity and you need to act now);
- A "very special" contact network in forex—(i.e., Cooper knows people who know forex; therefore, not everyone has access to the valuable information Cooper can get—that is what makes him so successful); and
- Cooper is living a lavish life and making "$30 thousand to $300 thousand each day"—(i.e., Cooper is getting rich from his own investing knowledge and you can get rich, too).[10]

explained in seminars and video conferences that he needed "deaf investors' monies to get his business going."[9]

The question that begs to be answered is: Why did Cooper need "deaf investors' monies to get his business going" if he was already making $30 thousand to $300 thousand each day? The answer: because Cooper and the scheme were fraudulent.[10]

Billion Coupons and Cooper's scheme were brought to the attention of state and federal regulators by a potential investor (the complainant) who had known Cooper for many years.[11] "[T]he deaf community is a small world," said the complainant to State of Hawaii investigators. Cooper met prospective customers through his representation of the Deaf Pilots Association at sponsored events such as the Deaf Fly-In Show and separately on a trip to Japan during which he conducted a series of twelve presentations about being a deaf, licensed pilot.[12] Cooper also operated his own nonprofit sign language organization, the Hawaii Sign Language Festival.[13] The activities Cooper participated in for the benefit or promotion of the deaf community went a long way to establish people's trust of Cooper within that community. In an affinity fraud, it is not only important to be seen as "one of us," but also to be seen as a prominent and respected member within the community.

All of the solicitations and facts mentioned here were used in the case against Cooper. During the Salt Lake City seminar, a Billion Coupons representative proclaimed that he had invested $21,000 himself in November 2007, and he would soon be receiving a check for close to $30,000. When the complainant was skeptical and asked that the representative send a copy of the check to him once he received it, the representative did so the following month. This was convincing, and the complainant was ready to invest $10,000 with Billion Coupons. However, when the

> **COMPLAINANT**—*A person who complains about violation of law and brings it to the attention of enforcement or adjudicatory authorities*

representative said, "You'll regret [it] if you don't invest with BCI [Billion Coupons, Inc.] because you won't become a millionaire in [a] few years . . ." a red flag went up that put the complainant off. He later commented to the Hawaii investigator, "Wow, that was a strong statement that [name redacted] made so I haven't made an investment with BCI yet because it sounded too good to be true."[14]

The Hawaii State investigation led to investigations by the CFTC and the SEC. Cooper switched gears and decided to cut ties with all new investors. He advised current representatives and investors to refrain from requesting monthly interest payments, advising them that if they left their money in Billion Coupons, in five years the fund would reach the $1 million mark.[15]

Cooper didn't have that long. Despite his attorney's representations that, "Mr. Cooper never solicited any funds" and that he "fell victim to his own success," Cooper was making preparations to leave the country for Panama. However, he had at least one prospective "representative" waiting in the wings to keep his business afloat.[16]

As Cooper planned his getaway, the CFTC, SEC, and Securities Commissioner of the State of Hawaii closed in. On February 18, 2009, all three filed actions against Billion Coupons and Cooper (the defendants). The CFTC's action alleged that Cooper and Billion Coupons ran a Ponzi scheme in which they solicited approximately 125 deaf American and Japanese customers for the sole purported purpose of trading forex. The defendants solicited $4.4 million but only deposited approximately $1.7 million into accounts that traded forex and on-exchange futures contracts, of which more than $749,000 was lost trading and more than $920,000 was withdrawn from the trading account and placed into Billion Coupons company accounts. The defendants misappropriated over $1.4 million of investor funds. As of the date of the CFTC and SEC lawsuits, only $30,000 was left in the accounts. As in every Ponzi scheme, in order to conceal their fraud, the defendants returned approximately $1.5 million to customers as purported "profits" and as commissions to its representatives and issued false account statements misrepresenting the purported value of customer accounts.[17]

The court appointed a *receiver* to administer the estate, recover customer funds, and distribute restitution to the defrauded investors. The receiver, along with CFTC attorneys, seized property pursuant to the court order. An inventory of Cooper's seized belongings included a home and condominium in Honolulu, two airplanes, one motorcycle, two electric motorbikes, two automobiles (including a 2005 Land Rover), office furniture, and computer equipment (six computers, three laser printers, and eleven flat-screen monitors).[18]

On July 29, 2009, the CFTC obtained a Consent Order of *Permanent Injunction* and *Other Equitable Relief* against Cooper barring him from trading commodity futures and options contracts and CFTC-regulated *foreign currency contracts* and prohibiting him from soliciting funds for such trading, registering with the CFTC, and acting as a principal, agent, or employee of a CFTC

RECEIVER—*Person appointed by a court to retrieve misappropriated assets*

DEAF INVESTORS	PROMISED RETURNS	SOLICITED FROM INVESTORS
125	15-20% MONTHLY	$4,400,000
LOST IN TRADING	**APPROX. MISAPPROPRIATED**	**DISGORGEMENT**
$749,000	$1,400,000	$6,200,000

registrant.[19] The agency received an order of summary judgment on August 26, 2010, and Cooper was ordered to pay $6.2 million in *disgorgement* and penalties. The complainant is a hero; his due diligence and complaint to the appropriate authorities likely saved hundreds of potential victims in the United States and Japan from losing their life savings to Billion Coupons and Cooper.

PERMANENT INJUNCTION—Order to stop violations of the Commodity Exchange Act or CFTC's rules

OTHER EQUITABLE RELIEF—Order for an accounting and gathering of misappropriated property gained by wrongdoing

FOREIGN CURRENCY CONTRACTS—Trading based on changing values of currencies

DISGORGEMENT—Money paid by wrongdoer based upon gain to wrongdoer

THREE

We Want You to Get to Know Us

Michael A. Kardonick and Atwood & James, Ltd.

"Our people: With 30 years experience, our team of 5 analysts, 4 strategists, and over 30 brokers serving clients all over Western and Central Europe. Our people are dedicated to the success of you, our customers. We spend more time with each client, offering a premium service. At Atwood & James, we take care of our brokers, and they stay with us a long time. Why do we take such care—not just because we're good people (though we are)—but because we know that a satisfied employee does his best for the company. And that's what we see in our brokers— they do their best for themselves, for us, and for you."

From the now defunct Atwood & James, Ltd. website[1]

Atwood & James, Ltd. liked to be seen as a small but sophisticated New York City-based global enterprise specializing in close relationships with its clients. With a Harvard grad, Michael Kardonick, at the helm, a company crest, and claims of a thirty-year virtually spotless trading history, Atwood & James appeared ready to deliver on those 90 percent annual profits it promoted on a risk-free basis.[2] But in fact, Atwood & James was a bogus forex investment scheme operated out of Rio de Janeiro by convicted felons. On May 18, 2010, Kardonick pled guilty in federal court to *conspiracy* to commit *money laundering* with his partner Gary Shapoff, using Atwood & James as their cover.[3] As part of his plea, Kardonick admitted that none of the investor proceeds were used for foreign currency transactions and that Kardonick and Shapoff took over $2.5 million from their customers for personal use.[4]

CONSPIRACY—*When two or more people join together to engage in illegal activity*
MONEY LAUNDERING—*Criminal cover-ups of money made through illegal activity*

Atwood & James created the illusion of a legitimate company by marketing itself through an elaborate website, advertisements in well-respected magazines including SkyMag, mail flyers, and through powerful personal solicitations.[5] The website detailed the extensive record and history of Atwood & James, a British company incorporated in New York State with offices in Rio de Janeiro, Amsterdam, London, and New York City.

In order to suggest a strong European presence, Atwood & James identified itself with a crest and included "Ltd." in its name, which, though used in the United States, is the British Commonwealth term for incorporation.[6] In case clients questioned the legitimacy of Atwood & James, the website had an answer prepared under the Frequently Asked Questions section of its site. The answer to "How do I know that I am dealing with a legitimate company?" claimed, among other things, that while Atwood & James' advisors and principals were not required to be licensed to trade the foreign currency options they were soliciting clients to trade in, they "have been licensed through various governmental agencies at one time or another in the past most still are."[7] That convoluted and grammatically incorrect answer dodges the question entirely.

When Michael Kardonick, the self-identified president and head analyst/trader, contacted potential clients directly, he boasted that Atwood & James was the only licensed and registered company in the foreign currency options trading industry with thirty years of experience and referred to friends in US politics, financial regulation, and on Wall Street. Kardonick and his cohorts also pitched an Atwood & James "*straddle*" trading strategy that was profitable regardless of market direction and ultimately prevented investments from being "lost," telling one prospective investor that if he ever lost his investment he'd be the "unluckiest trader in history." Indeed, Atwood & James' strategy was so invulnerable to loss that prospective clients were instructed to strike, as unnecessary, certain risk disclosure provisions in the Atwood & James Customer Advisory Agreement and highlight statements that emphasized the higher probability of profits based on the straddle strategy.[8]

After becoming an Atwood & James client, correspondence came in the form of confirmations on Atwood & James, Ltd. crested letterhead. The *confirmations* were practically bare; other than the client's name and account number and the date and details of the trade, there was little evidence of any transaction. There was no information as to the exchange on which the transactions were traded, no clearing firm or counterparty information, nothing but the name Atwood & James, Ltd.[9]

The uninformative confirmations from Atwood & James, Ltd. were part of the scam perpetrated by Kardonick, who, in reality, is a lifelong criminal. Kardonick served sentences three times in the 1970s for the sale and distribution of narcotics and for weapons possession. In 1989, he was convicted of fraud for selling bogus entries into a government lottery for oil and gas drilling licenses in Florida. In 1996, he was convicted of grand larceny for misusing customer credit card information. Kardonick does not, as claimed, hold a Harvard MBA.[10]

STRADDLE—*A trading strategy using companion trades or "legs"*
CONFIRMATION—*A statement from a broker setting forth terms of a trade*

Atwood & James, Ltd. is little more than a cyberspace fiction. Though registered as a New York corporation in the past, Atwood & James has never been registered with the CFTC in any capacity. There are no Atwood & James offices in New York City, Amsterdam, or London. There is an address for an office in a Rochester, New York, strip mall, but it is actually a retail clothing store; the phone number goes to the home of Shapoff, Kardonick's partner. Shapoff colluded with Kardonick in his 1989 fraud and was also a recipient of multiple federal convictions for mail and wire fraud. To date, no evidence of trading on US exchanges (or anywhere else) by Atwood & James has been found, nor is there evidence that Atwood & James ever opened or controlled any trading accounts. The client confirmations were blank because there were no exchanges, no clearing, and

PHANTOM OFFICES	ACTUAL OFFICE
AMSTERDAM, LONDON, NYC	RIO DE JANEIRO
BOGUS CREDENTIALS	ACTUAL CREDENTIALS
HARVARD M.B.A.	LIFE-LONG CRIMINAL
ADVERTISED PROFITS	ACTUAL LOSSES
90% YEARLY	TBD

no counterparties involved. Atwood & James and Kardonick used client funds—but not for their clients. Kardonick had personal trading accounts that sustained losses of approximately $1.7 million. Kardonick also directly used some of the money for himself and his family. When he did pay Atwood & James clients "profits," he was paying them with other clients' money in the traditional manner of a Ponzi scheme.[11]

Those who turned over their cash and their hopes to Atwood & James were victims. While there were numerous red flags along the way, such as lack of registration with any regulatory body, they were somewhat difficult to see. The Atwood & James website presented the appearance of a legitimate company, and the pricey advertisements, personal calls from the head of company, and the Atwood & James letterhead all contributed to the façade of a sophisicated investment company.

Following its filing of a civil complaint, on January 23, 2009, the CFTC obtained a federal court order in Rochester, New York, freezing the assets of Atwood & James, Kardonick, and Shapoff.[12] The case is ongoing against all defendants and has been stayed pending the completion of the related criminal action.[13] Kardonick's criminal sentencing is currently scheduled for September 2011.[14] During his plea hearing, when asked why he scammed people,

Kardonick responded, "What can I say? It was greed."[15] That was, at least, one honest statement.

FOUR

Ossie: An Extraordinary Liar

CRE Capital Corporation and James Ossie

"The damage done by this fraudulent investment scheme is extensive, leaving a trail of victims in its wake. These victim investors placed their trust in Mr. Ossie and now are literally paying for this misplaced trust."

— FBI Special Agent in Charge Gregory Jones[1]

CRE Capital Corporation (CRE) was a boutique, "invitation-only" financial firm that invested in foreign currency contracts. For a minimum investment of $100,000, one could join this exclusive club and receive guaranteed earnings of 10 percent every thirty days on the investment (woo hoo!).[2] CRE also allowed investment contracts in higher amounts of $300,000, $500,000, $1 million, $5 million, and $10 million. If investors couldn't afford these amounts, they were allowed to pool their funds to meet the threshold.[3] Like other scams, it was said there was no risk of loss. CRE claimed it held cash in a "reserve" account sufficient to repay all customers their investments plus the 10 percent monthly profit.[4] When questioned about how CRE could afford to pay investors 10 percent or more guaranteed interest each month, Ossie just told them he was a very skilled currency trader.[5] In reality, Ossie was not a skilled currency trader, but he was an extraordinarily skilled liar.

Ossie started CRE in early 2007.[6] Incredibly, in less than a year he successfully raised close to $28 million from over 120 different investors, largely through a group of salespersons, referred to as "correspondents," located throughout the United States.[7] Many, if not all, of the correspondents were investors in the "30 Day Currency Trading Contracts."[8] They received commissions based on bringing in first-time investors, and on top of that, earned commissions every time these investors renewed their contracts for another thirty days.[9] Furthermore, CRE was known to provide additional compensation to its correspondents, like an increased guaranteed monthly rate of interest of 20 percent (double the normal guarantee rate of 10 percent).[10] High incentives to go from investor to correspondent may have induced one correspondent to solicit an individual to invest $200,000 that he was using to fund his young daughter's cancer treatments in hopes that the guaranteed returns would help cover the costs.[11] While the CRE correspondents patted themselves on the back for the "positive effects" of "helping that family,"[12] Ossie knew the truth about CRE's real status.

Ossie was not a particularly good trader. In fact, during its nine-month life, CRE lost over $12 million investing in forex.[13] However, Ossie was diligent about wiring his investors their promised 10 percent every month with the knowledge that customers often rolled for another thirty days because of the guaranteed

MINIMUM INVESTMENT	GUARANTEED RETURNS	INVESTOR DEPOSITS
$100,000	10% MONTHLY	$27,899,975
APPROX. PHANTOM PROFITS AND COMMISSIONS	LOST IN FOREX TRADING	POCKETED BY OSSIE
$13,600,000	>$12,000,000	$1,800,000

continued profits.[14] As the "profits" came in, CRE's investors had no reason to question where the money was coming from, nor was there any incentive to remove their funds from Ossie's control.

While investors probably should have questioned the integrity of a business that claimed to provide its customers with consistent 10 percent monthly returns regardless of the profitability of trades, they did not. The returns appeared to be good, and CRE provided the comprehensive services that one would expect of an investment firm. Ossie organized regular conference calls among his current correspondents and prospective investors during which he shared his most recent strategies and successes. Ossie claimed that he hired outside accountants and auditors to ensure the integrity of the company's finances. Through their assigned correspondents, Ossie provided investors with unique log-ins and passwords to access their CRE accounts online and watch the profits roll in.[15]

But CRE Capital was a textbook Ponzi scheme. The chance to take part in an exclusive money-making opportunity with all the features of a genuine investment firm outweighed the CRE customers' good senses. A guaranteed 10 percent monthly return equates to at least a 120 percent annual return. Not only was a 120 percent return on investment worthy of a thorough explanation, it was also worthy of a phone call to the authorities. One call to the CFTC would have revealed that neither Ossie nor CRE was ever registered, a huge red flag. As for the use of outside accountants, Ossie never actually allowed those accountants access to trading account records.[16] Furthermore, the personal online accounts were created in their entirety to perpetuate the fraud. The reserve fund was also fiction. Indeed, by the end of 2008, CRE owed over $23 million on pending investments, but had just over $2 million in all of its bank and trading accounts combined.[17]

The court-appointed receiver has determined that investor deposits with CRE totaled $27,899,975. Ossie repaid investors approximately $2.6 million of their principal while paying out close to $7 million in fictitious monthly interest payments—the Ponzi part of this scheme. The correspondents received a whopping $4 million in commissions. Ossie took close to $1.8 million for himself, purchasing an $88,000 BMW, real estate, and jewelry, as well as making about $340,000 in credit card payments and $336,000 in payments to another one of his companies. He also blew over $300,000 on recreational boating and other goods and services like pet lodging.[18]

On May 21, 2009, James Ossie pled guilty to defrauding customers of nearly $25 million.[19] On July 30, 2009, Ossie was sentenced to six years and ten months in federal prison, to be followed by three years of supervised release, ordered to serve 250 hours of community service, and ordered to pay restitution in the amount of $18 million.[20]

On November 30, 2010, the Honorable Judge Richard W. Story of the United States District Court for the Northern District of Georgia entered a final judgment as to Ossie and CRE in the CFTC's civil case. In addition to the $4.8 million civil monetary penalty imposed on Ossie, the CFTC netted awards for restitution and a civil monetary penalty against CRE in the amounts of $5.7 million and $15.2 million, respectively.[21]

Ossie currently resides at the United States Penitentiary in Atlanta, Georgia, as prisoner #03476-036. As a result of the CFTC's civil case, Ossie can kiss his days of forex (and commodity) trading good-bye forever and instead contemplate how he's going to pay off the civil monetary penalty awarded in the CFTC case on top of the $18 million in criminal restitution.

FIVE

The Un-Coolest Guy in the Room

Charles "Chuck" Hays and Crossfire Trading, LLC

"Brutally honest, Chuck believes traders should first understand their individual strengths and limitations and trade accordingly. A very generous trader, Chuck has counseled and coached scores of futures traders in his own free time. Due to his natural Midwestern modesty and nonchalance, Chuck tends to downplay his accomplishments. He is, however, one of the best risk takers in the retail trading game."

—Excerpt from *Millionaire Traders*, Chapter 4:
The Coolest Guy in the Room[1]

When Bruce Hendry expressed an interest in investing on behalf of his family's charitable foundation in the fall of 2007, a friend directed him to day trader Charles "Chuck" Hays and his investment company, Crossfire Trading, LLC (Crossfire). This friend had invested his retirement money with Hays and Crossfire and had been receiving monthly checks at a return rate of approximately 3 percent, with no losing months. Drawn by the notion of high and seemingly risk-free returns, Hendry contacted Hays directly. Hendry went to Hays' home to discuss investment options for his family's charitable foundation and to catch a glimpse of the master trader in action. Impressed with what he saw, Hendry wired $2 million dollars of his own money and $1 million from the Hendry Family Foundation to a Crossfire account for the purpose of trading commodity futures in the Crossfire *commodity pool*. Several months later, based on reports from Hays, Crossfire account statements, and information pulled from Crossfire's password-protected website showing that he and the Family Foundation were earning consistent profits, Hendry wired an additional $2 million of his own money. Hendry invested a total of $5 million for all accounts.

About a year went by and Hendry began to wonder about his "too good to be true" investment that returned continuous profits, both on paper and in the form of sizeable disbursement checks. Hendry visited Hays at his home again, and Hays explained, for the first time, that Crossfire trades through an account at Dorman Trading, a registered futures commission merchant, and pulled an account statement on Dorman letterhead directly from an envelope that appeared to have just been received. Hays further explained that Crossfire had been introduced to Dorman through NDx Futures, Inc., a registered

COMMODITY POOL—*An arrangement in which multiple traders put their money together for group trading in commodities markets*

introducing broker. Now that Hendry had confirmed that his investments were being handled through registered, regulated companies, he felt he had done his due diligence. However, his doubts remained, and a few months later, he was back at Hays' house.[2]

This time, Hendry challenged Hays, asking him exactly where his money was and how it was being traded. Hays dodged Hendry's questions and showed Hendry another recent Dorman account statement for the entire Crossfire pool showing over $37 million at Dorman, with over $900,000 in profits for that month alone. Looking carefully at the statement, Hendry noted that there were no listings for fees, and he had noticed that the other account statements he had received also did not list fees, which seemed unusual. Hays told him just to trust him.[3]

The truth was that rather than investing in futures, Chuck Hays used Hendry and the Family Foundation's money on a $4 million luxury yacht.[4] Chuck Hays was not only a fraud, he was running a Ponzi scheme. Chuck Hays was so adept that even the industry bought into his scam. In their 2007 book, *Millionaire Traders*, Boris Schlossberg and Kathy Lien interviewed Chuck Hays as one of twelve "regular people" who have "hit it big" trading for themselves.[5] Schlossberg and Lien dub Hays "The Coolest Guy in the Room," praising him as "one of the best risk takers in the retail trading game," a guy who "often wins by violating some of the most sacrosanct rules of trading" yet thrives in the "chaotic world of E-mini stock index futures, where the difference between fortune and failure can be measured in seconds."[6]

To be fair to Schlossberg and Lien, Hays did trade. In fact, that is how he was able to conceal the fraud. Hays had an account at Dorman introduced by NDx Futures, but it was a personal account, opened in his own name in 2006. The account number for that account was one digit off from the Dorman account that appeared on the Crossfire account statements that Hays passed off to his clients; Hays doctored real Dorman account statements to appear as if they were for Crossfire.[7] Over the years Hays funded his personal Dorman trading account with as much as $2 million, only to close it in July 2008 with a balance of $300,000.[8]

On February 5, 2009, the CFTC filed a civil complaint against Hays for fraud, material misrepresentations, and operating a commodity pool without registering. That same day, Hays was arrested in his home state of Minnesota.[9] A few months later, on April 14, 2009, he pled guilty to criminal charges in connection with running a Ponzi scheme. As part of his plea agreement, Hays agreed to forfeit all assets procured through his offenses, which included the yacht as well as an array of other vehicles, jewelry, cash, and property.[10] The government estimates that investors lost more than $20 million in the scheme.[11] The Hendry money represents a quarter of that sum.

On April 27, 2010, Hays was sentenced to 117 months (almost ten years) in prison, ordered to pay $21,825,090 in restitution and $7,850 in victim attorney fees, and ordered to serve three years of supervised release following his prison term.[12] In the CFTC's civil case against Hays and Crossfire, the court granted the agency's motion for summary judgment and awarded the agency everything it asked for—$19 million in disgorgement and a $64 million dollar civil monetary penalty, as well as imposing a permanent trading ban on Hays.

HAYS' JAIL SENTENCE	RESTITUTION TO BE PAID BY HAYS	VICTIMS' ATTORNEY FEES TO BE PAID BY HAYS
117 MONTHS	$21,825,090	$7,850
DISGORGEMENT	**CIVIL PENALTY**	**HAYS TRADING STATUS**
$19,000,000	$64,000,000	BANNED PERMANENTLY

SIX

It Was Just a Loan!

Daren Palmer and the Trigon Group, Inc.

"It's not about revenge. It's about making sure it doesn't happen again to other people. It's something that needs to be closed; there's a lot of people who have been harmed on a lot of different levels—the least of which is Daren Palmer and his family."

—David Taylor, President, Taylor Chevrolet, Trigon Investor[1]

He was the high school quarterback who married his college sweetheart. He fathered five children and became an active leader in his ward of the Church of Jesus Christ of Latter-day Saints. He coached junior high football, instilling confidence and a sense of duty to "be the best son/brother/student" you can be.[2] However, in January 2009, he—Daren Palmer—disclosed to Idaho state authorities that he had been operating what amounted to a massive Ponzi scheme.[3]

Despite his admission to authorities, Palmer was adamant that the business he was running, the Trigon Group, Inc., was not an investment scheme. When asked by investigators about Trigon's investors and the nature of the funds they provided, Palmer stated, "They were lenders to me. They lent me the money."[4] Throughout his sworn testimony, Palmer talked about individuals "giving" and "lending" him money to use in his own trading program.[5] Rather than the typical customer advisory agreements, account opening documents, and disclosures, there were promisory notes for which Palmer posted no collateral.[6] The notes held a promise and understanding that Palmer would trade the borrowed funds in commodity futures and essentially split profits with the lender, with at least some guaranteed rate of return.[7] This distinction between "lenders" and "investors" is actually a key to under-standing how Palmer was able to carry out his operation for so long. Palmer never was registered to trade futures in commodity pools or hedge funds or to run a securities business and was, there-fore, completely off of the regulatory radar.[8] He didn't disclose this fact to his "lenders," and when asked point-blank by investigators whether he was aware of the registration requirement attached to engaging in futures and securities trading, Palmer replied, "The people had lent me money and that [sic] I did with it as I—as what we had agreed to do in the promissory note, which is to provide a return."[9] Unfortunately, the way he provided a return was to pay "lenders" with other "lenders'" money.[10]

Throughout the Idaho community that held him in such high regard, Palmer promoted himself as a successful investor with a complex trading strategy that generated consistent annual returns through investments in, among other things, commodity futures, options, and S&P 500 Index Futures.[11] Through neighbors and friends, his network of investors grew rapidly. By 2009, Palmer had collected more than $68 million from over fifty-five individuals and local entities.[12] In promissory notes and verbal promises, Palmer guaranteed some investors 20 to 40 percent in annual returns (and others as much as 7 percent monthly returns).[13] In exchange for these astonishing monthly returns, Palmer paid himself a salary ranging from $25,000 to $35,000 every month.[14] Although it appeared to investors that Palmer kept his promise of paying his clients 7 percent monthly returns on their investment, he was merely passing funds from new investors to earlier investors like a quintessential Ponzi scam.[15]

Palmer raised at least $68 million from clients and has admitted that only a fraction of that money, about $6.8 million, actually made it into trading accounts where it was eaten up in commissions and transactional fees.[16] Palmer sent more than $49 million in payments back to his investors.[17] The remainder of the cash was spent on the construction of two houses—one in the Canterbury Park neighborhood of Idaho Falls and one on the lake in Coeur d'Alene, Idaho—a fleet of automobiles, pricey jewelry, credit cards, and top-of-the-line snowmobiles.[18] Some of the Trigon money went to flimflam artist George Heffernan to "help trade" the funds.[19] Heffernan received approximately $15,000 to $25,000 a month from the Trigon funds in fees alone.[20] George Heffernan is a repeat offender whose latest misconduct—fraud involving, among other things, the sale and marketing of trading advice for S&P 500 and Nasdaq futures contracts, as well as two commodity futures trading methods—cost him $650,000 in sanctions.[21] Even when Palmer was trying to do what he promised, he failed miserably.

CLIENTS	GUARANTEED RETURNS	APPROX. AMOUNT COLLECTED
55	20–40% ANNUALLY	$68,000,000

Despite his claim that he was "borrowing" the money from his clients, Palmer made clear to his clients, in fairly unambiguous terms, that he would be pooling their money, trading it every day, and generating consistent returns because he could make money whether the market went up or down.

James Grey* lived on the same street as Palmer. After they became friends, Grey inquired about investing with Trigon. Palmer promised Grey that once his investment reached $1 million, Grey would earn a 25 percent annual return. Grey turned over the first of twenty-five investments with Palmer. Ultimately, Grey gave Palmer over $5 million and lost $3.5 of that to the Ponzi scheme. The payments he received steadily for years dried up by mid-2008, and when he demanded the return of funds to purchase a home, Palmer started making excuses about funds being flagged under the Patriot Act and being inaccessible in overseas accounts.[22] Palmer was digging himself into a hole of debt and was left with few options.

In late 2008, like a gambler who needs to "get back," Palmer made a hasty last ditch effort to, in his own words, "work my way out from underneath the incredible mess that I was in."[23] Palmer flew to London to meet with a group of complete strangers about a potential investment in Dubai.[24] Over several months, Palmer sent at least $500,000 in "fees" to this group hoping to secure additional funds that would allow him to dig himself out of his problems.[25] Not surprisingly, Palmer never heard from these alleged African and Middle Eastern investors again. At least some of the funds ended up in a Nigerian bank account, the kind you are always warned against sending money to when you get those suspicious emails from people in trouble.[26] Palmer had been scammed himself and the money was gone. "It's just humiliating,"

---

* This name has been changed to protect the privacy of the individual.

Palmer admitted. "It's embarrassing . . . just a nightmare."[27] In a reversal of fortunes, Daren Palmer was now the unwitting investor being swindled by con artists.

With few reasonable options left, Palmer turned himself into the authorities. Everything has been confiscated: the houses, land, jewelry, cars, horses, artwork, a grand piano, and the snow-mobiles.[28] An auction held in September 2009 at a warehouse previously owned by Palmer netted approximately $22,000 through the sale of furniture, jewelry, and other household items.[29] In the press, it was reported that even the children's stuffed animals and Christmas ornaments were carried away as a local restaurant hawked $5 barbecue to feed the crowd.[30] Palmer's now ex-wife is surviving on $2,000 a month from the receiver in exchange for her assistance in recovering Palmer's money.[31] As of January 6, 2011, $3,293,031 had been collected by the receiver for disbursement to the victims.[32]

On October 4, 2010, the district court issued an order of summary judgment against Palmer requiring him to pay $20,619,981 in disgorgement to victims and a civil monetary penalty of $20,619,981.[33] At least Palmer has some idea as to how it feels to be a victim of fraud. That is its own kind of punishment.

——— ———

SEVEN

I'm a Believer

George Hudgins

"I lied about the returns, misrepresented the returns in order to buy more time to make the money back. It wasn't just because I was lying trying to get people to put money in so I could steal it. That never crossed my mind. I never in my wildest dreams thought I was stealing money. And I'll show you in a little bit that I don't think I was."

—George Hudgins[1]

On March 13, 2009, George Hudgins was sentenced to 121 months in prison and ordered to pay close to $71 million in restitution in connection with his operation of an $86 million Ponzi scheme. He operated this scheme out of a two-room office he built on his homestead in the small city of Nacogdoches, Texas.[2] In addition to the restitution, all of Hudgins' earnings will be monitored for decades in order to repay, as much as possible, the investors he defrauded. Hudgins won't be able to earn any money in the markets.

Following his prison sentence, the terms of his supervised release in effect bar him from all positions relating to financial investing, and the court order against him in the civil lawsuit brought by the CFTC permanently bars him from the commodity industry.[3] This will make it hard for Hudgins to pay the $15 million civil penalty assessed in the civil order against him.[4] Is he at all remorseful? Yes. Does he believe he did anything wrong? No.[5] Hudgins distinguishes himself from traditional fraudsters, noting that the typical Ponzi operator sets up the scheme to steal money. He, on the other hand, claims to have worked eighteen to twenty hours a day trading for his clients. But when faced with the question about the $71 million he took from clients to purchase everything from airplanes, antique autos, and Civil War–era antiques to three carat diamonds for the women he was wooing, Hudgins relied on a recent diagnosis of bipolar disorder, maintaining that his misconduct can all be attributed to a "major manic episode" that put him in an alternate reality.[6] However, even Hudgins acknowledged that it was ego that turned his legitimate business into a fraud.[7] According to Hudgins, as soon as he moved back to his hometown of Nacogdoches in 2001, he was immediately "inundated by people with money" who hoped he would be as successful with their money as he was with his own.[8] He claims he never tried to get folks to invest with him, but not wanting to disappoint, Hudgins accepted everyone's money.[9] Three years later, in 2004, Hudgins created a commodity pool to open trading accounts and trade futures through a registered futures commission merchant.[10] However, Hudgins neglected to register the commodity pool or himself as its operator with the CFTC or any other regulatory body.[11]

Hudgins claims that friends and family were throwing money at him for reasons that "never came from me." However, as early as June 2001 he used fraudulent solicitations, including promo packets, newsletters, and group presentations to persuade members of the community to keep their money in his commodity pool, which he claimed was wildly successful.[12] How successful was it? In a 2005 promotional packet for prospective clients called "Hudg-Investments <Making Money in a Bull or Bear Market>," Hudgins reported gross returns for the commodity pool as follows: 99 percent for 2000; 55 percent for 2001; 57 percent for 2002; 46 percent for 2003; 47 percent for 2004; and 8.13 percent for January, 2005.[13] Those returns were even more amazing, considering the commodity pool wasn't even in existence for four of those years!

In January 2007, Hudgins made a presentation during an annual meeting of investors and potential investors. Not only did he tout those big performance numbers for 2000–2004, but he added returns for 2005 and 2006 of 52.33 percent and 22.5 percent, respectively, in spite of the fact that the trading accounts suffered losses close to $20 million during those years. Hudgins admitted that he was not registered with the CFTC, but told his audience that this was because neither he nor the commodity pool was required to be registered. Hudgins also reported that the pool's investment portfolio was approximately $80 million. At the time, however, the net value of Hudgins' trading accounts—which had never appropriately been in the name of the commodity pool— was negative $100,199.[14]

A lot of folks were lured into Hudgins' fiction because he was a member of their community with a reputation for being religious, generous, and professional.[15] He was the goldenboy who left home, passed his CPA exam, made some money, and then returned to share his fortune. Hudgins reached out to his community, giving and lending money to folks so they could accomplish their own dreams of purchasing homes and attending school.[16] He used his accounting background to create and distribute official-looking monthly and quarterly newsletters entitled "The HudgReport", which showed the pool's performance in charts and graphs, discussed trends in the markets, and urged investors to use the IRS Form 1099s he prepared for them to report their short-term earnings from the commodity pool.[17] Because Hudgins was running a Ponzi scheme, some funds were paid out to investors as "profits" from his trading.[18] People believed him because those "profits" were documented by a CPA.[19]

If it all appeared too good to be true, Hudgins had that covered, too. In a high pressure sales tactic, Hudgins told some prospective investors that the pool was getting so big—$200 million big—that he was "fixing to shut [it] down" and "stop taking any more money . . . start paying out some profits," rather than continuing to reinvest.[20] But at least one prospective investor didn't buy what Hudgins was selling. That investor called the CFTC to ask about George Hudgins and his wildly successful commodity pool. The CFTC brought an action to shut Hudgins down almost immediately and to try to recover funds for investors.[21]

Of the $88 million invested with Hudgins, $17 million was paid out to investors as purported profits. Hudgins lost at least $28 million trading unsuccessfully in futures markets, but a larger portion of investor losses resulted from Hudgins use of their money to feed his self-indulgent lifestyle.[22] Hudgins used his investors' money to purchase a 269-acre ranch on the Angelina River outside of Nacogdoches, thirteen acres of timber, mineral rights, a fleet of classic sports cars, and a Beechcraft Baron airplane. He had a King Air Turboprop on order and was building a hangar for it when his Ponzi scheme collapsed. Ladies in New York, St. Louis, and Toronto received diamonds—one topping 3.2 carats—and jewelry from Hudgins, who may have charmed the ladies while wearing one of his twenty pairs of cowboy boots. The list of items located and seized by the receiver goes on (and on) for pages.[23]

In February of 2009, the receiver made a partial distribution totaling $24,017,404 to the victims of Hudgins' scheme, which represented 33.9 percent of approved claims. Thereafter, based on collection efforts following the first interim distribution, the receiver had cash on hand in the amount of $3,344,650.

The receiver collected an additional payment of $618,526 from Rosenthal Collins Group, LLC (RCG), the futures commission merchant that handled Hudgins' accounts, which is the disgorgement RCG agreed to turn over to the receivership. The disgorgement was the result of a settlement between the CFTC and Rosenthal Collins, announced on October 4, 2010, following the Commission's tenacious pursuit of all parties sharing responsibility for the investors' losses.

Thereafter, on October 18, 2010, the receiver petitioned the court to approve a final distribution in the amount of $3,928,000, which the court approved. The final distribution represents an additional 5.54 percent distribution for a total distribution to the victims of 39.4 percent.

In the end, by virtue of the CFTC's quick action upon learning of Hudgins and the work of the receiver, the Department of Justice, the FBI, and the Texas Rangers, the victims of this Ponzi scheme

APPROX. AMOUNT COLLECTED	LOST IN TRADING	PHANTOM PROFITS
$88,000,000	>$28,000,000	$17,000,000
PRISON SENTENCE	RESTITUTION ORDERED	FINAL DISTRIBUTION
121 MONTHS	$71,000,000	39.4%

will ultimately receive about 39.4¢ for every dollar they invested and lost with Hudgins.[24] That 39.4¢ is a phenomenal return in the world of Ponzi schemes, since misappropriated funds are often squandered in ways that make them impossible to recoup.

Hudgins, who now resides at the Federal Correctional Institution in Butner, North Carolina, maintains that had the CFTC never caught on to his scheme, he would have turned it all around and made all the money he had promised. After all, according to Hudgins with regard to his newsletter, "Everything in there was true except the returns."[25]

EIGHT

The Magician

Joseph S. Forte

"AND NOW, this 16th day of March, 2010, it is ORDERED that Counsel for the Receiver and the Securities Exchange Commission shall FORTH-WITH provide the Court with a list of the currentlyknown "red flags" that arguably should have alerted investors to the fraudulent activities of Joseph Forte, L.P.

AND IT IS SO ORDERED."

Paul S. Diamond, Judge[1]

Joseph S. Forte was particularly good at making things disappear. However, he was not a magician, but a money manager who used smoke and mirrors to trick investors into thinking that he could earn them from 20 percent to more than 36 percent annually on their investments.[2] Forte promised to take relatively small sums of money, strategically place them in the commodities futures markets, and turn them into substantial wealth. Over the course of nearly thirteen years, Forte successfully performed this act, solic-iting more than $78.5 million from over one hundred Philadel-phia-area clients.[3] When Forte surrendered to federal authorities in December of 2008, all of the investors' money had disappeared. Although some of the money surfaced as "interest payments" and redemptions, millions of dollars had been transformed into the accoutrements of Forte's lavish lifestyle and into generous dona-tions to nonprofits. When the show was over, the funds were gone and it was clear that Forte was just a charismatic illusionist.

It all began back in 1995 when Forte and three others pooled about $200,000 to form a limited partnership with the purpose of investing in security futures.[4] Forte became the general managing partner of the limited partnership, Joseph Forte L.P., because of his self-certified success in trading commodity futures.[5] Over the next thirteen years, Forte built on his alleged success, bilking millions from investors eager to become new limited partners in his unreg-istered commodity pool, a pool that Forte promised would make colossal returns from trading futures in the S&P 500, treasury bonds, foreign currency, and precious metals.[6] By the time Joseph Forte L.P. filed its 2007 US Return of Partnership Income, it had over one hundred limited partners. The partners were completely unaware that Forte, the only individual who had authority to make day-to-day decisions concerning the operation of the partnership, had been operating it as a Ponzi scheme from day one.[7]

Where did all the money go? Other than the quarterly fraud-ulent account statements that Forte conjured up and passed through an accountant—who happened to be one of the original three limited partners—he had little to show for his success as an investor. In fact, from 1998 through 2008, he lost more than $3 million trading commodity futures. From October 2004 through July 2007, Forte barely traded at all, and from October 2002 through February 2007, Forte didn't deposit any funds in the commodity pool's trading account.[8] Following the Ponzi format, Forte used investor money to pay both interest and principal to some investors, while the rest went directly to his own accounts. Forte paid himself generous management and incentive fees based on the artificial value he attributed to the commodity pool.[9] Forte used these funds to build his stature, or rather his façade, in the community.[10] In addition to purchasing multiple cars, jewelry, and a beach house on the Jersey Shore, Forte invested in at least sixteen small businesses and was wildly generous to area charities.[11]

How did this scheme grow so large and endure for so long? Well, it ballooned and sustained itself because investors were not only receiving quarterly statements from an accountant showing that the value of the commodity pool had grown to over $154 million, but they were receiving actual returns. Plus, investors were paying taxes on those returns, because Forte made sure that everyone received federal tax forms setting out their taxable profits from the commodity pool.[12]

Forte's act seemed too good to be true, but by creating a complete fiction, it was hard for regulators and investors to discover the truth. Throughout the scam, Forte never registered with any regulatory body, nor were his quarterly account statements ever properly vetted by an independent accountant. Only

CLIENTS >100	PRISON SENTENCE 15 YEARS
AMOUNT COLLECTED >$78,500,000	APPROX. RESTITUTION $35,000,000
LOST IN TRADING >$3,000,000	PENALTIES $35,000,000

when news of the Madoff scandal hit did some investors begin to question Forte about the health of the commodity pool and request the return of their investments. Unable to make additional payments without soliciting new investors, Forte came clean with authorities.[13] Of the original $78 million, it remains unclear how much will ultimately materialize. In an attempt to recover as much as possible, the court has appointed a receiver to assist in selling the houses, cars, and jewelry. In addition, the investors who received fictitious profit payments will, in all likelihood, be forced to return them. Even the nonprofits will have to return the donations. These funds were never Forte's to give.[14]

> **BANK FRAUD**—*Criminal fraud against a bank to obtain a loan or other bank services*

As for Forte, he pled guilty to wire fraud, mail fraud, *bank fraud*, and money laundering charges in June of 2009. In November of that same year, Forte was sentenced to a term of fifteen years imprisonment with five years of supervised probation and ordered to pay close to $35 million in restitution and another $35 million in penalties.[15,16] In the CFTC's case against Forte, a permanent injunction is in place, and the receivership is in the process of collecting funds and determining the amount of restitution owed to investors.

Forte now resides in the Metropolitan Detention Center in Brooklyn, New York. Joseph S. Forte turned into federal inmate #63656-066; he's projected to reappear in 2023.

NINE

A Car to Match Every Outfit

Sean Healy

"In reality, Healy simply used the investors' funds to live a lavish lifestyle, purchasing millions of dollars of luxury items such as a $2.4 million mansion furnished with over $2 million in improvements, $1.5 million in men's and women's jewelry, numerous exotic vehicles and performance sports cars, including a Bentley, Ferraris, Lamborghinis, and Porsches worth over $2.3 million, and employing a team of bodyguards, drivers, nannies, and maids to serve him and his family on a daily basis."

—Excerpt from the indictment against Sean N. Healy[1]

In July 2009, the CFTC charged Sean Nathan Healy of Weston, Florida with defrauding investors of over $14 million. Healy falsely claimed that he would use their money to trade, among other things, commodity futures contracts and commodity options contracts on their behalf. Contrary to Healy's claims, he did not use any of these funds for investments; rather, Healy went on a spending bender with his wife Shalese, whose profession as a Hooters waitress became media fodder during this case.[2]

Healy first graced Florida with his presence in 2001. He left New York after the investment firm he worked for, Guru Investment, closed upon commencement of an investigation into its trading activities. Despite just turning the corner of his thirtieth birthday, Healy's story was that he had retired to Florida after making millions of dollars on Wall Street and selling his investment firm for somewhere in the range of $30 to $40 million. He told people that he was still day trading stocks and commodities for enormous profits, but that this wasn't making him happy— he wanted his friends, family, and even acquaintances to make money along with him.[3]

Though investigators have tracked Healy's fraud as far back as 2003, Healy ramped up his activity beginning in May 2008. In order to lure investors—who, according to Assistant US Attorney Bruce Brandler, included his own unsuspecting mother and mother-in-law—Healy represented that he owned or had access to numerous shares of stocks in companies like Ruth Chris. He claimed these shares were valuable because they were "restricted," that is, not generally available to the public. At times, he used financial terms like "options" or "warrants" in describing these purported equities, claiming that he could sell the shares to his investors at a huge discount. According to Healy, when the shares became "unrestricted" in a few months' time, they would become extremely valuable and return huge profits upon sale. Healy also represented that he continued to trade stocks and futures from his home computer and participated in investment partnerships like "Pride Rock" with investors "Matt," "Andy," "Rich," and "Mike."[4]

By investing with him, Healy promised that investors could share enormous wealth.

Throughout the scheme, Healy repeatedly assured investors that his futures and options trading was earning excellent returns and that distributions of tremendous trading profits would be made in February 2009. Healy, however, never provided investors any detail or documentation regarding what investments he made, what brokerage accounts he had, and who the other participants were in his partnerships. This was the biggest red flag: no conventional forms of documentation were ever provided to investors.[5] There were no trade confirmations, brokerage account statements, or stock certificates. Instead, Healy provided verbal assurances, emails, phony account statements, and for the most part, handwritten statements purporting to show successfully traded futures and options.[6] In addition to the handwritten statements, Healy consistently told investors that he achieved only trading successes, stating on one particular occasion, "this is almost too easy . . . there's times and this is one of the few times in your life that you're going to see oil go up like this, therefore, you have to take advantage of the opportunity because this only happens like [sic] a once in a lifetime."[7]

To get the funds he needed to keep the fraud going, Healy directed investors to wire funds directly to bank accounts in Florida or to write checks payable to the entities he controlled. The bank accounts were all in the name of Shalese, which should have raised another red flag. Healy, however, had this covered. He told investors he kept all of his assets and accounts in Shalese's name in order to conceal them from his ex-wife.[8]

For the record, Healy didn't retire to Florida at the age of thirty with millions in the bank. His tax returns for 2001 show that he reported a total income of less than $23,000 and a loss of $5,000 for his sale of Guru Investments stock. His income was negative for 2004–2007. As for the stock sales, commodity futures trading, investment partnerships, and Matt, Andy, Rich, and Mike, there is no evidence that Healy did any of this or that these people even existed.[9]

During the time that Healy received money from investors, he and Shalese used the funds to create the lavish lifestyle consistent with the story Healy was telling. The Healys purchased the $2.4 million Weston mansion formerly owned by football legend Bernie Kosar and spent another $2 million on home furnishings and home improvements, including Versace crystal, built-in safes, built-in stereo systems, at least seventeen plasma televisions, a $500,000 theater screening room, smart-house wiring and panels, and video surveillance systems.[10] In addition to an entire room dedicated to watching sports on five plasma televisions, the Healys collected over fifty pieces of sports memorabilia, including a signed Brett Favre #4 New York Jets jersey and a Joe Frazier autographed boxing glove.[11]

Someone in that house also liked music. The inventory of items purchased by the Healys included Stratocaster guitars signed by the Doobie Brothers and Fergie and "The Ultimate Grammy Collection" Epiphone Guitar signed by such legends as Bruce Springsteen, Madonna, Paul McCartney, and BB King.[12] The Healys purchased a fleet of luxury vehicles in colors such as lime green and "blue & cream," including multiple Ferraris, Lamborghinis, Porsches, a Bentley, a Maserati, a Saleen, a Lincoln Limousine, and of course, a metallic burnt-orange Hummer golf cart.[13] They purchased approximately $1.4 million in watches and other jewelry laced with diamonds and precious stones, including brands such as Rolex, Piaget, Patek Philippe, Hublot, Paris Hilton, Gregg Ruth, and Levian Couture.[14] He also converted the invested funds into gold and silver bullion and coins.[15] Healy used investor money to lease 2,500 square feet of garage space to store the vehicles, pay for an exclusive country club membership, and lease luxury suites at the Bank Atlantic Center Arena for sporting and other entertainment events.[16]

Occasionally, investors received money. Healy sometimes paid investors "profits" or returned part of their investments using funds obtained from other investors in signature Ponzi style.[17]

The Healys' binge was short-lived. When February 2009 rolled around, Healy told investors that the futures and options trading account, which allegedly had a $79.3 million balance, was temporarily restricted because certain transactions "were still open." By March 2009, Healy told investors that "regulatory issues" had reduced the value of the account and that only distributions of principal would be available. These statements were, of course, false since no trading actually occurred and no such account ever existed. Investors finally had enough, and a fraud action was initiated against Healy and his wife on March 16, 2009, in the US District Court for the Southern District of Florida.[18]

The US Attorney's Office for the Middle District of Pennsylvania (USAO), the district where the majority of investors resided, became aware of the fraud action and began a federal grand jury investigation.[19] During the course of the investigation, Healy lied to his attorney and federal investigators by furnishing numerous falsified documents, including fictitious affidavits, bank records, and brokerage account records from a representative named "Mike Hein" at a firm called PCF and for an account he claims to have maintained at Interactive Brokers (Interactive), a futures commission merchant registered with the CFTC.[20] PCF is not a registered futures trading firm or broker-dealer, and the purported address on the PCF documents produced to the USAO is nonex-

INVESTOR DEPOSITS	PRISON SENTENCE	RESTITUTION
>$14,000,000	188 MONTHS	$16,773,995

istent. Likewise, there is no record of any registered representative by the name of "Mike Hein" or "Michael Hein" at any firm registered with the CFTC or SEC. The phone number for customer assistance listed on the PCF account statements was listed to a "Mark Hein," email address mhein54@yahoo.com. The grand jury investigation revealed that Healy, or someone acting on his behalf, purchased a prepaid wireless cell phone on April 6, 2009, from a convenience store near Healy's Florida home and created the email address to corroborate the false story that Healy gave the very next day during his sworn deposition.[21]

In October 2009, Healy was indicted in the Middle District of Pennsylvania for multiple counts of wire fraud, mail fraud, money laundering, and *obstruction of justice*.[22] On November 23, 2009, Healy pled guilty to two counts of wire fraud and one count of unlawful monetary transaction, and was released on conditions including electronic monitoring and participation in a substance abuse evaluation. Between November 23, 2009 and December 2, 2009, Healy violated bail twice: once by failing to adhere to the instructions of the US Pretrial Services Office with regard to remaining in his supervisory residence while awaiting installation of monitoring equipment, and once for his continued use of controlled substances. Just one week into his supervised release, Healy went missing, turned up, submitted to a drug test, and tested positive for the presence of cocaine, opiates, benzodiazepine, and amphetamines.[23] By January 7, 2010, Healy was in custody.[24]

On March 31, 2010, Healy was sentenced to 188 months imprisonment (about 15½ years), $16,773,995 in restitution,

OBSTRUCTION OF JUSTICE—*Hindering or interfering with law enforcement and investigations*
RELIEF DEFENDANT—*A nominal party to a proceeding who is expected to give up ill-gotten gains or property innocently held as a result of a co-defendant's wrongdoing*

and three years supervised release. Healy's prison wages will be garnished for restitution.[25] Mr. Healy, prisoner #16444-067, hasn't given up yet; he appealed his sentence to the United States Court of Appeals for the Third Circuit.[26]

On June 22, 2010, the US District Court for the Middle District of Pennsylvania entered a consent order of permanent injunction, including disgorgement, a civil monetary penalty, and equitable relief against Sean Healy and his company, Sand Dollar Investing Partners, LLC. The order, among other things, permanently bars Healy from engaging in any commodity-related activity. It also orders Healy to pay disgorgement in the amount of $14,637,000 and an additional penalty in that same amount, $14,637,000.[27] On April 26, 2011, the court granted the CFTC's motion for summary judgment against Shalese Healy as a *relief defendant* and ordered her to pay disgorgement in the amount of $14,637,000.[28]

An Unfortunate Loss

Barki, LLC and Bruce C. Kramer

"Ryan passed away on Tuesday, June 23, 2009, in peace at his home, after a strong courageous battle against cancer. He was born October 31, 1973, in Charlotte, the son of Don Puckett and Rhonda Kramer. . . . Ryan is survived by his loving wife and high school sweetheart, and their infant daughter."

—Excerpted from Ryan Puckett's obituary by the *Charlotte Observer*[1]

Ryan Puckett was Bruce Kramer's stepson. He battled cancer for more than three years and was blessed with a daughter in late 2008. Unfortunately, Ryan spent his last months submitting to a deposition and coming to terms with the fact that he had unknowingly brought himself, his family, and many of his friends into Kramer's scheme. Ryan took money from his own retirement fund, the fund that could have one day taken care of his daughter, to provide start-up money for what would become his stepfather's $38 million Ponzi scheme.[2] With no life insurance and an obligation to pay back the receiver all the false profits he unknowingly obtained, Ryan passed away leaving his loved ones with both an emotional and a fiscal loss.

Bruce Kramer never ended up in prison for his fraud. On February 25, 2009, Rhonda Kramer, his wife and partner (in name only) to his company, Barki, LLC, heard the gunshot as she entered their home, having ignored his last telephone call as she pulled into the driveway. Bruce Kramer had locked himself in his home office and committed suicide. He never submitted to a deposition, never had to face his own wife, never had to tell a single investor that their money was gone, and never could be held accountable for the lives he destroyed. However, on top of his desk, Kramer left a paper trail to follow.[3]

When lawyer A. Stuart McKaig organized Barki in 1999 as a *limited liability company* with two members, Bruce and Rhonda Kramer, he had thought its intended purpose was to administer Rhonda's health insurance. McKaig's role was limited, and though he ceased having anything to do with Barki other than to remain its registered agent, he had close ties to Rhonda, whom he employed as a legal secretary for fifteen years, and to Ryan's wife Diana*, whose mother had also worked for him. It was McKaig who came to Rhonda and Ryan's aid in the days following Bruce's demise. As he drove over to the Kramer home, McKaig received a call from Diana who said she and Ryan had been getting calls from investors. Knowing that Ryan was ill and that he had a three-month-old daughter, McKaig told her to have the investors call him, which they did by the dozens.[4]

---

* This name has been changed to protect the privacy of the individual.

LIMITED LIABILITY COMPANY—A form of business organization that shields business owners from personal responsibility for the organization's debts

When McKaig entered Bruce's office on February 27, he found two sets of approximately fifty to sixty of Barki's 2008 Form K-1s, tax forms used by partnerships to report income. One set, he recalled, was dated January 2009, and the other set of amended Form K-1s was dated February 2009. Much to McKaig's surprise, the Form K-1s contained the names and addresses of various partners for Barki with capital contributions in the millions and partner capital contributions and earnings in the tens of millions. McKaig was surprised because he thought that the only members of Barki were Bruce and Rhonda. McKaig also found a Combined Account Statement purporting to be from Forex Capital Markets, LLC (FxCM), a registered futures commission merchant. The statement appeared to have been dated February 19, 2009, and purported to show an account balance for Barki of $61 million.[5]

Not long after, a North Carolina attorney representing several Barki investors contacted McKaig about the Barki accounts. McKaig and Rhonda Kramer learned directly from FxCM that as of that day, March 3, 2009, there were four Barki accounts, but only one was active and had a balance of about $575,000. The FxCM account statement found by McKaig on Kramer's desk just a few days before was fraudulent, as were multiple purported FxCM account statements produced by the North Carolina attorney from his clients. Indeed, Mr. McKaig and Mrs. Kramer learned that during the entire life of the Barki accounts, neither the account balances nor the deposits ever totaled an amount over

$59 million; the actual deposits into the Barki accounts collectively totaled approximately $17.6 million.[6]

The next day, March 4, 2009, McKaig contacted the CFTC.[7] The CFTC filed a complaint against Barki, LLC and Bruce Kramer as defendants, and Rhonda Kramer and Forest Glen Farm, LLC as relief defendants and secured a statutory restraining order, which, among other things, froze the defendants' and relief defendants' assets and authorized the appointment of a receiver to begin the process of locating and marshaling assets.[8]

The charges in the complaint were simple: since at least June 2004 through February 2009, the defendants fraudulently solicited no less than $38 million from at least seventy-nine individuals or entities for the purported purpose of trading off-exchange foreign currency on their behalf. In doing so, the defendants sustained massive trading losses, operated a Ponzi scheme, and pocketed millions of investor dollars. Kramer, who claimed to be an expert mathematician, told investors and prospective investors that his trading software allowed him to evaluate market trends and situations and successfully trade without ever having a losing month and without ever losing a single dollar of principal. Additionally, Kramer stated that his system involved very little risk and that his only fee would be a percentage based upon the investors' earnings. Investors executed a trading agreement with Barki which, among other things, provided that all funds would be traded through Barki and that investors would receive monthly statements and a year-end Form K-1 showing any profits or losses allocated to investors.[9]

Between January 2003 and September 2008, Kramer opened four trading accounts at FxCM in the name of Barki. Of the more than $38 million solicited by Kramer, only the $17.6 million made it into the Barki trading accounts. Contrary to his representations, Kramer was not successful in his trading, and the accounts suffered losses almost every single month for about a six-year time period totaling over $10 million. Kramer withdrew about $6 million from the trading accounts. He misappropriated the rest to pay purported profits or return principal to Barki investors in classic Ponzi fashion and to finance Rhonda's and his personal expenses. Those personal expenses included a 48-acre horse farm and 6,000 square foot residence, luxury automobiles, artwork, a Belgian jumper horse (including the equine passport required to import him), and extravagant parties. Kramer covered it all by paying purported profits to investors and by providing them with assurances including fraudulent account statements consistently showing monthly profits of 3 to 4 percent and Form K-1s demonstrating that Barki had never experienced a losing month.[10]

Mrs. Kramer denies any involvement in or knowledge of Kramer's wrongdoing, and Kramer left a suicide note corroborating Rhonda's innocence as to his activities with Barki.[11] Unfortunately, Rhonda's faith in her husband's trading talents, coupled with her position and reputation in their tightly knit horse country community, made her an innocent lure for new investors. Like many Ponzi schemes, this one was an affinity fraud.

For example, until 2006, Bob and Susan Greene* owned Forest Glen Farm in Midland, North Carolina. The Greenes met Rhonda almost a decade before when she began boarding a horse at Forest Glen. Over the years, they became friends and learned all about Barki and Kramer's limited risk strategy that turned Ryan's $50,000 investment into a cool $1 million in just a few years. Susan's mother, impressed by what she heard through her

---

* Names have been changed to protect the privacy of the individuals.

daughter, invested in Barki in 2005, received monthly statements showing highly positive trading results, and withdrew funds during the life of the investment. That was all the Greenes needed to see, but they had a problem because Barki required a $250,000 minimum investment. Not wanting to miss out, the Greenes sold the Kramers a little less than half of the 110-acre farm and a house on it to raise that initial investment. Over the years the Greenes invested about $350,000 total, with their last investment just one month before Kramer took his own life. They were consistently able to make withdrawals and received high earnings statements and Form K-1s showing annual profits as high as $143,000. Their experience was so positive that they brought in several other investors, including the Reeds.[12]

Mike and Jenifer Reed** boarded a horse at Forest Glen when it was owned by the Greenes and met the Kramers through the horse farm connection. Though they moved their horse off the farm when it changed hands, the Reeds became interested in investing in Barki after the Greenes told Mike Reed about their never-ending winning streak. With the understanding that the minimum investment was $250,000, Mike Reed met with Bruce Kramer in person. Kramer told him that the minimum investment was now $500,000. Reed indicated that he only had $300,000. Kramer assured him that as soon as he had the money Barki would love to have him as an investor. Kramer told him that he had been a math professor at Virginia Tech, which Reed felt was the right background. Although Reed "didn't understand exactly how he did the Barki trading," Kramer explained that currency trading was a good investment because while stocks could be going down, currencies weren't tied to specific economic trends, and he could

_____

** Names have been changed to protect the privacy of the individuals.

INVESTORS	MINIMUM INVESTMENT
>79	$250,000
TOTAL INVESTOR DEPOSITS	**LOST IN TRADING**
>$38,000,000	>$10,000,000

"play all the cards" at once. Kramer explained that he had thirty to forty investors and was working with $60 million.[13]

In January 2009, Susan Greene told Mike Reed that Bruce Kramer was contemplating raising the minimum investment to $1 million. The Reeds decided to invest "quickly before the minimum was raised," and secured the necessary funds by acting on a *power of attorney* Jenifer Reed had for her mother, whose investments she managed. In five separate wire transfers, the Reeds sent Barki about $659,000 ($500,000 of that came through the power of attorney). Bruce provided a receipt on February 1, 2009, dated February 2, 2009. Reed emailed Bruce shortly thereafter to inform him that his mother-in-law had passed away and that the limited liability company he had set up to invest in Barki, which would now include his brother-in-law, might be interested in investing more money later. Bruce responded in an email, expressing his condolences and stating that, naturally, it would not be a problem if his brother-in-law wanted to add more money to Barki later.[14]

Bruce Kramer accepted funds and reassured the Barki investors up until the end that he was no Bernie Madoff. We will never know if Kramer set out to run a Ponzi scheme, or if he was trying to run a legitimate forex trading business that never panned out. Had he not taken his own life, Kramer's house of cards would have fallen soon. There would have been a civil action, and, very likely, a criminal one. A receiver would still have been appointed, and all the assets of Barki gathered and sold. The victims still would be angry. Even

POWER OF ATTORNEY—*Legal authority that enables a person to act on someone else's behalf.*

the "net winners" who, through the benefit of the Ponzi scheme, received Barki withdrawals in excess of the principal amount of their investment cannot simply walk away. Since those funds were fraudulent transfers rather than "profits," the winners, like Ryan's widow, must return them to the receiver or face litigation.[15] In addition, thanks to Kramer's extra attempts to create legitimacy, the fraudulent Form K-1s caused victims to report their fictitious profits for tax purposes. Now the victims must deal with the IRS to rectify their tax returns.[16] Many are expected to receive refunds. In the case of Ryan, who gained about half a million dollars, his estate has agreed that 80 percent of the tax refunds from the federal and state taxing authorities will be turned over to the receivers.[17]

Had Kramer come clean to authorities, he might still be around to answer the difficult questions, sort out the mess, and take the blame that has been levied against Rhonda, Ryan, and others.

EPILOGUE

In addition to providing a look into the world of Ponzi schemes, the past ten chapters should have tipped you off that financial frauds persist and infiltrate communities of all kinds. We are all at risk of being defrauded. Persons of any level of intelligence and financial sophistication are vulnerable to experienced con artists. The scamsters use tricks not only targeted at undermining our knowledge and ability to make rational economic decisions, but aimed at our own humanity. There is no shame in being a victim of fraud. Fraudsters are smart and calculating in the methods used to gain your confidence and your cash.

There is something you can do: educate yourself. Through financial education you can understand how to avoid fraudulent and financially inappropriate or destructive transactions. Financial education is the first line of defense against a variety of unsuitable, unfair, and unacceptable practices in the marketplace. Most importantly, financial education empowers you to exercise your consumer protection rights.

Unbelievably, fraudsters even exploit financial education, so be careful. Anyone can create an Internet website, pay for an advertisement, or put on a seminar claiming to provide the keys to savvy investing, so you need to be smart about how and where you get your information. The best unbiased financial education materials are put out by federal and state financial regulators and congressionally authorized self-regulatory organizations like the National Futures Association (NFA) and the Financial Industry Regulatory Authority (FINRA). Not only can you be certain that these materials are accurate, but you can be sure that no one will be soliciting you to hand over your hard-earned cash at the end.

NEXT STEPS

Because commodity futures and options trading is one of the most complex and risky segments of the investment world, it is especially fertile ground for fraudsters. It's difficult to spot a fake when you don't even know what the real one looks like. In order to beat a con, you have to be able to pierce their façade by asking questions, getting accurate verifiable information, and seeking out the right people for help when you need it.

The following sections describe how you can avoid becoming a victim by knowing and using your rights as an investor, identifying some of the more common red flags of fraud, and knowing who to contact and where to go for additional information, assistance, and answers to any questions you may have regarding your past, current, or future investments.

Investors' Bill of Rights[1]

When you invest with anyone in any product, you have the right to:

Honesty in Advertising

Many individuals first learn of investment opportunities through advertising in a newspaper or magazine, on radio, television, the Internet, or by mail. Phone solicitations are also regarded as a form of advertising. In practically every area of investment activity, false or misleading advertising is against the law and subject to civil, criminal, or regulatory penalties.

Bear in mind that advertising is able to convey only limited information, and the most attractive features are likely to be highlighted. Accordingly, it is never wise to invest solely on the basis of an advertisement. The only bona fide purposes of advertising are to call your attention to an offering and encourage you to obtain additional information.

Full and Accurate Information

Before you make an investment, you have the right to seek and obtain information about the investment. This includes information that accurately conveys all the material facts about the investment, including the major factors likely to affect its performance.

You also have the right to request information about the firm or the individuals with whom you would be doing business and whether they have a track record. If so, you have the right to know what it has been and whether it is real or hypothetical. If they have been in trouble with regulatory authorities, you have the right to know. If a rate of return is advertised, you have the right to know how it is calculated and the assumptions on which it is based. You also have the right to ask what financial interest the seller of the investment has in the sale.

Ask for all available literature about the investment. If there is a prospectus, obtain it and read it. This is where the bad, as well as the good, about the investment has to be discussed. If an investment involves a company whose stock is publicly traded, get a copy of its latest annual report. It also can be worthwhile to check out the Internet or visit your public library to find out what may have been written about the investment in recent business or financial periodicals.

Obtaining information isn't likely to tell you whether or not a given investment will be profitable, but what you are able to find out—or unable to find out—could help you decide if it's an appropriate investment for you at that time. No investment is right for everyone.

Disclosure of Risks

Every investment involves some risk. You have the right to find out what these risks are prior to making an investment. Some, of course, are obvious. Shares of stock may decline in price. A business venture may fail. An oil well may turn out to be a dry hole.

Others may be less obvious. Many people do not fully understand that even a US Treasury Bond may fluctuate in market value prior to maturity—or that with some investments, it is possible to lose more than the amount initially invested. The point is that different investments involve different kinds of risk and these risks can differ in degree. A general rule of thumb is that the greater the potential reward, the greater the potential risk.

In some areas of investment, there is a legal obligation to disclose the risks in writing. If the investment doesn't require a prospectus or written risk disclosure statement, you might nonetheless want to ask for a written explanation of the risks. The bottom line: Unless your understanding of the ways you can lose money is equal to your understanding of the ways you can make money, don't invest!

Explanation of Obligations and Costs

You have the right to know, in advance, what obligations and costs are involved in a given investment. For instance, does the investment require that you must take some specific action by a particular time? Or is there a possibility that at some future time or under certain circumstances you may be obligated to come up with additional money?

Similarly, you have the right to a full disclosure of the costs that will be or may be incurred. In addition to commissions, sales charges, or "loads" when you buy and/or sell, this includes any other transaction expenses, maintenance or service charges, profit sharing arrangement, redemption fees, or penalties and the like.

Time to Consider

You earned the money and you have the right to decide for yourself how you want to invest it. That includes sufficient time to make an informed and well-considered decision. High pressure sales tactics violate the spirit of the law, and most investment professionals will not push you into making uninformed decisions. Thus, any such efforts should be grounds for suspicion. An investment that "absolutely has to be made right now" probably shouldn't be made at all.

Responsible Advice

Investors enjoy a wide range of different investments to choose from. Taking into consideration your financial situation, needs, and investment objectives, some are likely to be suitable for you and others aren't, perhaps because of risks involved and perhaps for other reasons. If you rely on an investment professional for advice, you have the right to responsible advice.

In the securities industry, for example, "suitability" rules require that investment advice be appropriate for the particular customer. In the commodity futures industry a "know your customer" rule requires that firms and brokers obtain sufficient information to assure that investors are adequately informed of the risks involved. Beware of someone who insists that a particular investment is right for you although he or she knows nothing about you.

Best Effort Management

Every firm and individual that accepts investment funds from the public has the ethical and legal obligation to manage money responsibly. As an investor, you have the right to expect nothing less.

Unfortunately, in any area of investment, there are those few less-than-ethical persons who may lose sight of their obligations and of your rights. They do this by making investments you have not authorized, making an excessive number of investments for the purpose of creating additional commission income for themselves, or at the extreme, by appropriating your funds for their personal use. If there is even a hint of such activities, insist on an immediate and full explanation. Unless you are completely satisfied with the answer, ask the appropriate regulatory or legal authorities to look into it. It's your right.

Complete and Truthful Accounting

Investing your money shouldn't mean losing touch with your money. It's your right to know where your money is and the current status and value of your account. If there have been profits or losses, you have the right to know the amount and how and when they were realized or incurred. This right includes knowing the amount and nature of any and all charges against your account.

Most firms prepare and mail periodic account statements, generally monthly. You can usually obtain interim information on request. Whatever the method of accounting, you have both the right to obtain this information and the right to expect that it be timely and accurate.

Access to Your Funds

Some investments include restrictions as to whether, when, or how you can have access to your funds. You have the right to be clearly informed of any restrictions in advance of making the investment. Similarly, if the investment may be illiquid—difficult to quickly convert to cash—you have the right to know this beforehand. In the absence of restrictions or limitations, it's your money and you should be able to have access to it within a reasonable period of time.

You should also have access to the person or firm that has your funds. Investment scam artists are well versed in ways of finding you, but particularly once they have your money in hand, they can make it difficult or impossible for you to find them.

Recourse, if Necessary

Your rights as an investor include the right to seek an appropriate remedy if you believe someone has dealt with you—or handled your investment—unfairly or dishonestly. Indeed, even in the case of reasonable misunderstandings, there should be some way to reconcile differences.

It is wise to determine before you invest what avenues of recourse are available to you if they should be needed. One means of exercising your right of recourse may be to file suit in a court of law. Or you may be able to initiate arbitration, mediation, or reparation proceedings through an exchange or a regulatory organization.

Red Flags of Fraud

Most folks give you ten, we'll give you twenty (And the tips that follow are free!)

1. "If it sounds too good to be true, it is." Always begin with this premise. Whatever the promise is, whether it is a monthly return of 3 percent or 30 percent, compare the promised profit yields to current returns on similar investments. Any investment opportunity that promises unreasonably high returns is likely both very risky and inappropriate for the average investor or is simply a sham.
2. The investment involves "little or no risk of loss" or promises that "no client will ever lose a single penny." All investments have some degree of risk. If there was really such thing as a riskless investment, do you think a fraudster would share it with you?
3. Profits or profit payments or rates of return on investment are guaranteed regardless of whether the investment actually

makes money or the direction of the markets. Remember those "reserve" funds that the Ponzi schemers set up so that profits were guaranteed? Well, they either didn't exist or were being funded with other investors' money. If you are told that you will be subsidized for any losing transactions or losing months or that you will not have any losing transactions booked to your accounts, don't buy it; 99.9 percent of the time it's illegal.

4. There is a need for secrecy. A refusal to provide written information about the investment and/or the salesperson or entity offering or managing it including the identity of any persons or entities involved in the investment, investment strategy, account statements, or handling of funds is a sign that there is indeed something to hide. You always should request that all information about the investment and the persons and/or business entities offering it be provided in writing. Legitimate persons and entities should have no problem providing such information; however, fraudsters may be unwilling to provide such materials due to the risk of exposure to legal action, regulatory authorities, or the truth that they are totally bogus. Whether your requests are flat-out denied or you receive excuses as to why the person/entity cannot comply with your request, their refusal should equate to your refusal of their offer.

5. The fees are based on your profits, fees are not written, or there are no fees at all. Fees should be clear and up-front and should not create an incentive for the investment manager to lie, cheat, or otherwise engage in conduct aimed solely at fee generation (this is usually referred to as "churning").

6. The investment is difficult to understand or incomprehensible. Good investment strategies should be logical and should not require complex explanations. Fraudsters often seek out victims

who are new to investing or who have little understanding of the type of investment being offered. Fraudsters may rely on their target's confusion to play up their own special skills and expertise. Or, they might be using such confusion to build up the target's confidence by making them think they understand when they do not. Ask questions until you understand the investment, and if you find that you need additional help, seek an independent person who you can trust such as an accountant or attorney.

7. You are discouraged from seeking an independent evaluation of the investment or the firm itself. If you are told that you don't need to get a second or independent opinion because the investment has already been audited or vetted by a CPA/auditor/attorney or because the individual you are talking to just happens to be any one of these professionals, be cautious. Remember, fraudsters often create false identities, companies, and documents to create legitimacy. Protect yourself by requesting all independent audits and reviews and getting the opinion of someone with verifiable credentials.

8. The firm or salesperson soliciting you to invest is not regulated nor registered with a state or federal regulatory body or claims that it is not (or they are not) subject to regulation or registration. There are few exceptions when it comes to the necessity to register and be regulated by a state or federal financial regulatory authority. If you are told that the firm or individual is not subject to registration or regulation, request additional details and contact the appropriate regulatory body for more information. Either way, it is important to understand what it means to be registered and regulated, and you should always do an independent check. Think about it: would you go to a surgeon who doesn't need to be licensed to practice medicine over one who is? Exactly.

9. The firm or investment strategy has never had a losing month or has had very few. Remember, there is no such thing as a sure thing. Be critical of visuals used to convey this same message. The profit or return line on a performance chart shouldn't consistently increase and, even if the chart is accurate, past performance is not indicative of future results.

10. The private placement memorandum, offering memorandum, or other offering documents contain minimum investment requirements or minimum investment experience levels and the general or managing partner is willing to waive either for you. If the firm is legitimate, it is required by law to abide by these limitations, which are often imposed through regulation and registration status. Minimum requirements generally correspond to the riskiest of the investment, so use this information to determine whether the particular investment is appropriate for you and your financial situation.

11. You are told to make the investment based on trust. Remember, this is your hard-earned money, and your trust in the persons who handle it should also be hard-earned.

12. You are pressured to make a decision immediately or within a limited time frame. No one wants to miss out on an opportunity, especially when it is an once-in-a-lifetime offer. However, if it is a good investment opportunity, it will still be there after you've done your due diligence.

13. You are told that the investment opportunity is only open to a limited number of people, certain people, only friends and family, or "the investment pool is so big, that it is just getting too profitable to manage, so really, I just need to shut it down and pay out some big profits"—you get the gist. This is another kind of high-pressure sales tactic. The creation of scarcity and promises of exclusivity make something appear more valuable than it is.

14. The firm or person needs your money to get/keep the investment going. If the investment is profitable, then it shouldn't need your money. Remember: Ponzi schemes always require increasing amounts of new money flowing in to pay off earlier investors and stay afloat.

15. The investment has abnormal, unfamiliar, or suspicious instructions for depositing or wiring money, or if you are already investing, the deposit or wiring instructions frequently change. If your money is on the move, the fraudster probably is too.

16. You receive testimonials that you cannot verify. Beware, the salesperson you are talking to may be just another part of the ruse.

17. You do an Internet search for the firm, investment, or salesperson and nothing comes up. If an investment is that good, folks will be writing, talking, and blogging about it. But remember, you cannot believe everything you read or see on the Internet, so if you do find information, make sure you independently verify its truth. Remember the international firm headquartered in a Rochester strip mall? Yup.

18. You receive an unsolicited offer or communication. Fraudsters often use unsolicited email and faxes to attract their victims. If you don't know the source of the offer or communication, throw it out/delete it.

19. The individual or firm you have invested with stalls you when you want to pull out your principal or profits, or you were withdrawing funds regularly and have been advised that you can no longer do so. If an investment has periods when you cannot withdraw your funds, you should be made aware of this information before you invest.

20. The salesperson asks for your credit card number "for identification" or information regarding your bank accounts.

This is not how one is identified; this is how one ends up with unauthorized credit card charges and a damaged credit rating that will stay with you for years.

This is a lot to remember, so if you are overwhelmed, simply remember what your parents told you when you were little:

"Do I know their mother?" (Red Flags 4, 7, and 8)

"If you don't know why you are doing it, don't do it" (Red Flag 6)

"Every question is a good question" (Red Flags 6 and 7)

"Just because everyone else is doing it . . ." or *"If everyone jumped off of the Brooklyn Bridge, would you?"* (Red Flags 11, 12, and 16)

"Don't take candy from strangers" (Red Flags 11 and 18)

"Everyone is special" (Red Flag 13)

"Just because it is on the TV, Internet, etc. doesn't mean it's real" (Red Flag 17)

Resources

If the investment involves futures or options on futures or forex:

Commodity Futures Trading Commission (CFTC)

www.cftc.gov
Three Lafayette Centre
1155 21st Street, NW
Washington, DC 20581
Phone: 202-418-5000
Report suspicious activities or transactions:
1-866-FON-CFTC (1-866-366-2382)
Fax: 202-418-5521
Email: Questions@cftc.gov

National Futures Association (NFA)

www.nfa.futures.org
300 S. Riverside Plaza, #1800

Chicago, IL 60606-6615
Phone: 312-781-1300
Fax: 312-781-1467

If the investment offer involves securities:

Securities And Exchange Commission (SEC)

www.sec.gov
100 F Street, NE
Washington, DC 20549
Phone: 202-942-8088
Investor information:
1-800-SEC-0330 (1-800-732-0330)
Investor education: www.investor.gov

Financial Industry Regulatory Authority (FINRA)

www.finra.org
1735 K Street, NW
Washington, DC 20006
Phone: 301-590-6500

Securities Investor Protection Corporation (SIPC)

www.sipc.org
1667 K Street N.W., Suite 1000
Washington, D.C. 20006
Phone: 202-371-8300

You can also contact your state's securities agency and find valuable investor education materials through:

North American Securities Administrators Association (NASAA)

www.nasaa.org
750 First Street, N.E., Suite 1140
Washington, DC 20002
Phone: 202-737-0900

Additional Investor Education Resources
Mymoney.gov

www.mymoney.gov
Phone: 1-800-FED-INFO (1-800-333-4636)
The US government's website dedicated to teaching all Americans the basics about financial education. Mymoney.gov is managed by the Federal Financial Literacy and Education Commission.

The National Fraud Information Center (NFIC)

www.fraud.org

The Cme Group: Education

www.cmegroup.com/education/index.html
Phone: 1-866-716-7274

Nyse Euronext: Investor Relations and Outreach

Investor Hotline: 1-800-218-1182

Options Industry Council

www.optionseducation.org
Phone: 1-888-OPTIONS (1-888-678-4667)

American Association of Retired Persons (AARP)

http://www.aarp.org/money
Phone: 1-888-687-2277

American Savings Education Council (ASEC)

www.choosetosave.org
Phone: 202-659-0670

Alliance For Investor Education (AIE)

www.investoreducation.org
AIE is dedicated to facilitating greater understanding of investing, investments, and the financial markets among current and prospective investors of all ages. AIE pursues initiatives for education and joins with others to motivate Americans to obtain objective information and increase their knowledge and understanding of investing.

American Association of Individual Investors

www.aaii.com
Phone: 1-800-428-2244

American Institute of Certified Public Accountants (AICPA)

www.360financialliteracy.org
Phone: 1-888-777-7077

Council for Economic Education

http://www.councilforeconed.org

Investor Checklist

The following checklist is designed to help you ask the right questions before making an investment. Once you get the answers, do your due diligence and verify the information with the appropriate federal regulator and with your state securities regulator. Remember, the time to ask questions is before you hand over your money.

Salesperson/Agent Information:
- *Salesperson/Agent Name*
- *Company/Business Name*
- *Company/Business Address*
- *Phone Number*
- *Website Address*

Investment Products/Services Offered:
- *Commodity Futures/Options*

- *Foreign Currency*
- *Securities*
- *Annuities*
- *Estate Planning*
- *Real Estate*
- *Insurance*
- *Other*

Who regulates or licenses the product/service offered?

What license(s) or registration(s) do you hold that authorizes you to offer or sell this product/service?

Write down the license/registration numbers for all applicable licenses/registrations.

What written information will I receive about this investment before I make a decision?

- *Offering or Private Placement Memorandum*
- *Prospectus*
- *Most Recent Annual Report*
- *Most Recent Quarterly or Interim Report*
- *Recent News Releases*
- *Research Reports*

What are the risks associated with this investment?

What are the fees and associated costs for this investment and how are they calculated?

Are there any restrictions on accessing funds once I invest?

Endnotes

1. Testimony of Harry Markopolos, CFA, CFE Before the H. Comm. On Fin. Servs. at 26 (Feb. 4, 2009).

CHAPTER ONE

1. *United States v. Diamond,* No. 09-cr-00586 (M.D. Fla. Nov.6, 2009) (order denying defendant's motion for reconsideration of the court's order of detention).
2. Complaint for Injunctive and other Equitable Relief for Civil Penalties under the Commodity Exchange Act pp. 32–33, *CFTC v. Diamond,* No. 09-cv-1811 (M.D. Fla. Sept. 3, 2009).
3. *Id.* p. 20.
4. *Id.* p. 21.
5. *Id.*
6. Complaint, *supra* note ii, p. 20; Indictment p.17, *Diamond,* No. 09-cr-00586 (M.D. Fla. Dec. 17, 2009).
7. Indictment, *supra* note vi, pp. 4, 17.
8. Plaintiff's Memorandum in Support of its Renewed Motion for Preliminary Injunction and Other Equitable Relief, Ex. 1 Declaration p. 2, *Diamond,* No. 09-cv-1811(M.D. Fla. Sept. 10, 2009).
9. Pl.'s Mem., *supra* note viii, Ex. 4 Decl. pp. 4–5.
10. Pl.'s Mem., *supra* note viii, Ex. 3 Decl. at Ex. A.
11. The program, 5Minute Forex™, was available on e-bay for $199.97. Fortunately, recent Internet searches indicate that it is no longer available.
12. Pl.'s Mem., *supra* note viii, Ex. 4 Decl. pp. 4–6.

13. *Id.* pp. 7–10.
14. *Id.* pp. 12–13, 19–20.
15. Pl.'s Mem., *supra* note viii, Ex. 1 Decl. p. 4, Attach. A.
16. *Id.*
17. Complaint, *supra* note ii, p. 27.
18. *USA v. Beau Diamond,* Case No. 09 Cr-586, United States District Court Middle District of Florida, Tampa Division, Dkt. 110, Verdict Form, July 21, 2010.
19. *Id.*, Dkt. 132, Criminal Judgment, December 22, 2010.
20. *U.S. Commodity Futures Trading Commission v. Beau Diamond and Diamond Ventures LLC,* Case No. 09 CV 1811, United States District Court for the Middle District of Florida, Tampa Division, Dkt. 59, Final Judgment Order of Restitution and Civil Monetary Penalty Against Defendants Beau Diamond and Diamond Ventures LLC, December 30, 2010.
21. Pl.'s Mem., *supra* note viii, Ex. 3 Decl. Attach. I.

CHAPTER TWO

1. Declaration of Temporary Receiver Barry A. Fisher in Support of Plaintiff Securities and Exchange Commission's Application for Preliminary Injunction and Appointment of a Receiver Ex. 5, *SEC v. Billion Coupons, Inc.,* No. 09-cv -00068 (D. Haw. Feb. 27, 2009) (Consolidated with *CFTC v. Billion Coupons, Inc.,* No. 09-cv-00069 (D. Haw. Feb. 18, 2009)).
2. Complaint for Permanent Injunction, Civil Monetary Penalties, and Other Equitable Relief p. 15, *Billion Coupons, Inc.,* No. 09-cv-00069 (D. Haw. Feb. 18, 2009).
3. Consent Order of Permanent Injunction and Other Equitable Relief against Defendant Marvin Ray Cooper p. 18, *Billion Coupons, Inc.,* No. 09-cv-00068 (D. Haw. July 29, 2009).
4. *Id.* p.15; Declaration of Curt K. Hasegawa in Support of Plaintiff Securities and Exchange Commission's *Ex* Parte Application for a Temporary Restraining Order Ex. 1 at 1, *Billion Coupons, Inc.,* No. 09-cv-00068 (D. Haw. July 29, 2009).
5. Consent Order, *supra* note iii, pp. 16, 19.
6. Decl. of Curt K. Hasegawa, *supra* note iv, Ex. 2 at 9–10.
7. *Id.* at Ex. 1 at 1, Ex. 2 at 10.
8. *Id.* at Ex. 2 at 10.
9. *Id.* at Ex. 2 at 9.
10. *Id.* at Ex. 2 at 9.
11. Decl. of Curt K. Hasegawa, *supra* note iv, p.9, Ex. 2.
12. *Id.* at Ex. 2 at 9–10, Ex.6 at 60.
13. *Id.* at Ex 2 at 11; *See also* http://www.taxexemptworld.com/organization. asp?tn=1573975.
14. Decl. of Curt K. Hasegawa, *supra* note iv, Ex. 2 at 9–10.
15. *Id.* at Ex. 5 at 39.
16. *Id.* at Ex. 6 at 60–64; Decl. of Barry A. Fisher, *supra* note i, Ex. 5 at 1–2; Plaintiff Securities and Exchange Commission's Reply Memorandum in Support of

Application for Preliminary Injunction at 2, *Billion Coupons, Inc.,* No. 09-cv-00068 (D. Haw. Feb 27, 2009).

17. Complaint, *supra* note ii, pp. 1, 27–28, 30.
18. Inventory of Receiver Exs. A, B, *Billion Coupons, Inc.,* No. 09-cv-00068 (D. Haw. Mar. 23, 2009).
19. Consent Order, *supra* note iii.

CHAPTER THREE

1. Plaintiff's Ex Parte Motion for a Statutory Restraining Order Ex. 8J, *CFTC v. Atwood & James, Ltd.,* No. 09-cv-06032 (W.D.N.Y. Jan. 23, 2009).
2. Complaint for Injunctive and other Equitable Relief for Civil Penalties under the Commodity Exchange Act p. 2, 22, 28, *CFTC v. Atwood & James, Ltd.,* No. 09-cv-06032 (W.D.N.Y. Jan. 22, 2009).
3. Plea Agreement pp. 1, 5, *United States v. Kardonick,* 10-cr-06068 (W.D.N.Y. May 18, 2010).
4. *Id.*
5. Complaint, *supra* note ii, p.19; Pl.'s Ex Parte Mot., *supra* note i, Exs. 2 p.5, 8J.
6. Complaint, *supra* note ii, pp. 21–23.
7. *Id.* p. 32; Pl.'s Ex Parte Mot., *supra* note i, Ex. 8J.
8. Complaint, *supra* note ii, pp. 33, 37, 44, 47–49.
9. *Id.* p. 51.
10. Criminal Complaint, Black Aff. pp. 4–6, 35, *United States v. Kardonick,* No. 09-mj-00562 (W.N.Y. May 7, 2009).
11. Complaint, *supra* note ii, pp. 14–15, 17, 56–58, and 61; Criminal Complaint, Black Aff., *supra* note x, pp. 11–13.
12. *Atwood & James, Ltd.,* No. 09-cv-06032 (W.D.N.Y. Jan. 23, 2009) (*Ex Parte* Statutory Restraining Order).
13. *Atwood & James, Ltd.,* No. 09-cv-06032 (W.D.N.Y. April 29, 2009) (Decision and Order).
14. *Kardonick,* No. 10-cr-06068 (W.D.N.Y. May 18, 2010) (Sentencing Guideline Order).
15. Brett Davidsen, *I-Team 10 Investigations: Multi-million $$ Investment Fraud,* WHEC TV, May 20, 2010.

CHAPTER FOUR

1. Press Release, U.S. Department of Justice, U.S. Attorney's Office, N. Dist. of Ga., Currency Fund Manager Pleads Guilty to Perpetrating Ponzi Scheme (May 21, 2009).
2. Complaint for Permanent Injunction, Civil Monetary Penalties, and other Equitable Relief p. 1, *CFTC v. CRE Capital Corp.,* No. 09-cv-0115 (N.D. Ga. Jan. 15, 2009); Complaint for Injunctive and Other Relief, *SEC v. CRE Capital Corp.* p.2, No. 09-cv-0114 (N.D. Ga. Jan. 15, 2009). (CRE *Capital Corp.,* Nos. 09-cv-0115 and 09-cv-0114 were consolidated.)

3. Complaint, *supra* note ii, p. 16, No. 09-cv-0115 (N.D. Ga. Jan. 15, 2009).

4. *Id.* p. 3.

5. Motion for Default Judgment as to Defendant James G. Ossie and Supporting Memorandum of Law at 2, *CRE Capital Corp.*, No. 09-cv-0114 (N.D. Ga. Apr. 6, 2009).

6. Complaint, *supra* note ii, p. 13, No. 09-cv-0115.

7. Mot. for Default J., *supra* note v, at 5, 8, 13.

8. *Id.* at 9.

9. *Id.*

10. *Id.*

11. *Id.* at Ex. 2.

12. *Id.*

13. Complaint, *supra* note ii, p. 3, No. 09-cv-0114.

14. Complaint, *supra* note ii, p. 17, No. 09-cv-0115.

15. *Id.* pp. 18–19, 23.

16. U.S. Department of Justice, U.S. Attorney's Office, N. Dist. of Ga., *supra* note i.

17. *Id.*

18. Mot. for Default J., *supra* note v, at 13–14, Declaration of Michael Fuqua pp. 6–11.

19. Department of Justice, United States Attorney's Office, Northern District of Georgia, *supra* note i.

20. Press Release, U.S. Department of Justice, Currency Fund Manager Sentenced to Nearly 7 Years in Federal Prison for Perpetrating Ponzi Scheme (July 30, 2009).

21. On April 19, 2010, the Honorable Judge Richard W. Story of the United States District Court for the Northern District of Georgia entered a Final Judgment as to Defendant James G. Ossie in the SEC's civil action against CRE and Ossie. Among other things, the Judgment finds Ossie liable for disgorgement of $1,793,925.95, representing profits gained as a result of his alleged misconduct, and a $25,000 civil monetary penalty. Final Judgment as to Defendant James G. Ossie, *CRE Capital Corp.*, No. 09-cv-0114 (N.D. Ga. Apr. 19, 2010).

CHAPTER FIVE

1. Kathy Lien & Boris Schlossberg, *Millionaire Traders: How Everyday People are Beating Wall Street at Its Own Game* 77 (2007). The 2010 edition of *Millionaire Traders* does not include the Chuck Hays chapter.

2. *Id.* pp. 23–25.

3. *Id.* pp. 25–26

4. *Id.* p. 31.

5. Lien & Schlossberg, *supra* note i, at VII.

6. *Id.* at 77.

7. Complaint, *supra* note ii, p. 27.

8. *Id.* pp. 28–29.

9. Press Release, U.S. Department of Justice, Minnesota Man Arrested in Connection with Ponzi Scheme (Feb. 5, 2009).

10. Press Release, U.S. Department of Justice, Minnesota Man Pleads Guilty to Running Ponzi Scheme (Apr. 15, 2009), *available at* http://www.justice.gov/opa/pr/2009/April/09-crm-352.html.
11. *Id.*
12. Press Release, U.S. Department of Justice, Minnesota Man Sentenced to 117 Months in Prison for Running a Ponzi Scheme (Apr. 27, 2010).

CHAPTER SIX

1. Andrew Del Greco, *Latest Report on Recovery of Daren Palmer's Assets for Ponzi Scheme Victims,* KPVI News 6, July 16, 2009.
2. Sven Berg and Clark Corbin, *Daren Palmer Revealed: The Rise, Riches and Ruin of One of Eastern Idaho's Most Prominent Characters,* Idaho Falls Post Register, November 8, 2009 at A1.
3. Complaint for Injunctive and other Equitable Relief and for Civil Penalties under the Commodity Exchange Act p. 6, *CFTC v. Palmer,* No. 09-cv-00076 (D. Idaho Feb. 26, 2009).
4. Memorandum in Support of Plaintiff's Motion for Summary Judgment Against Daren L. Palmer Ex. 2 at 29, *SEC v. Palmer,* No. 09-cv-00075 (D. Idaho Feb. 26, 2009).
5. *Id.* at 29–33, 52.
6. Complaint, *supra* note iii, p. 27; Mem. in Supp. of Pl.'s Mot. for Summ. J. Against Daren L. Palmer, *supra* note iv, Ex. 11.
7. Complaint, *supra* note iii, p. 28; Mem. in Supp. of Pl.'s Mot. for Summ. J. Against Daren L. Palmer, *supra* note iv, Ex. 2 at 32–35, Ex. 11.
8. Mem. in Supp. of Pl.'s Mot. for Summ. J. Against Daren L. Palmer, *supra* note iv, Ex. 2 at 51–52.
9. *Id.* at Ex. 2 at 52.
10. *Id.* at Ex. 2 at 66.
11. Mem. in Supp. of Pl.'s Mot. for Summ. J. Against Daren L. Palmer, *supra* note iv, p. 6–7.
12. Memorandum in Support of Plaintiff's Motion for Summary Judgment Against Daren L. Palmer 3, *Palmer,* No. 09-cv-00076 (D. Idaho June 17, 2010).
13. Complaint, *supra* note iii, pp. 27–30.
14. *Id.* p. 34.
15. *Id.* p. 35.
16. Mem. in Supp. of Pl.'s Mot. for Summ. J. Against Daren L. Palmer, *supra* note xii, at 5.
17. *Id.* at 6.
18. Complaint, *supra* note iii, p. 34.
19. Mem. in Supp. of Pl.'s Mot. for Summ. J. Against Daren L. Palmer, *supra* note iv, Ex. 2 at 49–50.
20. *Id.* at Ex. 2 at 85–86.
21. Press Release, U.S. Commodity Futures Trading Comm'n, U.S. District Court Orders George Heffernan, a/k/a George W. Marshall, to Pay $650,000 in Sanctions

in Federal CFTC Action Involving Fraudulent Commodity Trading Advice and Services (Apr. 9, 2008).

22. Mem. in Supp. of Pl.'s Mot. for Summ. J. Against Daren L. Palmer, *supra* note iv, Ex. 7 pp. 2–7.

23. Mem. in Supp. of Pl.'s Mot. for Summ. J. Against Daren L. Palmer, *supra* note iv, Ex. 2 at 87.

24. *Id.* at Ex. 2 at 89.

25. *Id.* at Ex. 2 at 89–91.

26. *Id.* at Ex. 2 at 88.

27. *Id.* at Ex. 2 at 87. 28

28. Third Report of R. Wayne Klein, Receiver (For Period Ending September 30, 2009) at 8, *Palmer,* No. 09-cv-00076 (D. Idaho Oct. 26, 2009).

29. *Id.*

30. Berg and Corbin, *supra* note ii.

31. Third Report of R. Wayne Klein, *supra* note xxviii, at 6.

32. *Id.* at 12.

33. On June 17, 2010, the CFTC filed a Motion for Summary Judgment against Palmer. Motion for Summary Judgment Against Daren L. Palmer, *Palmer,* No. 09-cv-00076 (D. Idaho June 17, 2010).

CHAPTER SEVEN

1. Matthew Stoff, *Daily Sentinel Interview with George Hudgins,* The Daily Sentinel, May 30, 2009.

2. United States v. Hudgins, No. 08-cr-00027 (E.D. Tex. Mar. 31, 2009) (Judgment in a Criminal Case).

3. *Id.*; CFTC v. Hudgins, No. 08–00187 (E.D. Tex. 2009) (Consent Final Order of Permanent Injunction, Civil Monetary Penalty and other Equitable Relief).

4. *Id.*

5. Stoff, *supra* note i.

6. *Id.*

7. Matthew Stoff, *Inside the Mind of George Hudgins,* The Daily Sentinel, May 30, 2009; Stoff, supra note i.

8. Stoff, *supra* note i.

9. *See id.;* Consent Order, *supra* note iii, p. 16.

10. Consent Order, *supra* note iii, p. 14.

11. *Id.*

12. *Id.* p.15.

13. Complaint for Permanent Injunction, Civil Monetary Penalties, and Other Equitable Relief p. 20, *CFTC v. Hudgins,* No. 08-cv-00187 (E.D. Tex. May 13, 2008).

14. *Id.* pp. 24–27.

15. Stoff, *supra* note i.

16. Initial Report of the Receiver at 11–12, *Hudgins,* No. 08-cv-00187 (E.D. Tex. July 8, 2008).

17. Consent Order, *supra* note iii, p. 22; Information at 3, *Hudgins,* No. 08-cr-00027 (E.D. Tex. July 21, 2008).

18. Consent Order, *supra* note iii, pp. 24–26.
19. *Id.* p. 24; Stoff, *supra* note i.
20. Complaint, *supra* note xiii, p. 35.
21. Stoff, *supra* note 1.
22. Consent Order, *supra* note iii, pp. 2(c), 26.
23. Initial Report of the Receiver, *supra* note xvi, at 2–11; Second Report of the Receiver at 5, *Hudgins,* No. 08-cv-00187 (E.D. Tex. Sept. 3, 2008).
24. Fifth Report of the Receiver at 3, *Hudgins,* No. 08-cv-00187 (E.D. Tex. May 11, 2009).
25. Stoff, *supra* note i.

CHAPTER EIGHT

1. *SEC v. Forte,* No. 09-cv-00063 (E.D. Pa. Mar. 16, 2010) (Order). (Consolidated with *CFTC v. Forte,* No. 09-cv-00064 (E.D. Pa. Jan. 8, 2009)).
2. *CFTC v. Forte,* No. 09–00064 (E.D. Pa. Sept. 30, 2009) (Consent Order of Permanent Injunction and Other Equitable Relief against Defendant Joseph S. Forte p.9).
3. Second Report of Marion A. Hecht, Court-Appointed Receiver for Joseph S. Forte and Joseph Forte, L.P. at 1, Ex.2, *Forte,* No. 09-cv-00064 (E.D. Pa. Mar. 1, 2010).
4. Consent Order, *supra* note ii, at 4–5.
5. Complaint for Permanent Injunction, Civil Monetary Penalties, and Other Equitable Relief pp. 15–16, *Forte,* No. 09-cv-00064 (E.D. Pa. Jan. 7, 2009).
6. Consent Order, *supra* note ii, at 5.
7. Second Report of Receiver, *supra* note iii, at 1.
8. Consent Order, *supra* note ii, at 7.
9. *Id.*
10. *Id.* at 8.
11. Second Report of Receiver, *supra* note iii, at 11–16.
12. Consent Order, *supra* note ii, at 7.
13. Second Report of Receiver, *supra* note iii, at 1.
14. Second Report of Receiver, *supra* note iii., at 10, 22–14.
15. Press Release, FBI - Philadelphia Division, U.S. Department of Justice, Delaware County Man Sentenced to 15 Years for Multi-Million Dollar Investment Scheme (Nov. 14, 2009).
16. On September 30, 2009, the U.S. District Court for the Eastern District of Pennsylvania entered a consent order of permanent injunction against Forte barring him from trading commodity futures and options contracts and CFTC-regulated foreign currency contracts, and prohibiting him from soliciting funds for such trading, registering with the CFTC and acting as a principal, agent or employee of a CFTC registrant. The order also requires payment of restitution to defrauded pool participants and a civil monetary penalty the specific amounts of which will ultimately be determined in the near future by the court-appointed Receiver. Consent Order, *supra* note ii.

CHAPTER NINE

1. Indictment p. 6, *United States v. Healy,* No. 09-cr-0319 (M.D. Pa. Oct. 9, 2009)
2. Gus Garcia-Roberts, *Moron of the Week: Self-Destructive Ponzi Baller Sean Healy,* Miami NewTimes Blog, October 30, 2009.
3. Indictment, *supra* note i, pp. 1, 3, 6.
4. *Id.* pp. 4–5.
5. *Id.* p.8.
6. *Id.* pp. 7–8
7. Complaint for Injunctive and other Equitable Relief and for Civil Monetary Penalties under the Commodity Exchange Act p.22, *CFTC v. Healy,* No. 09-cv-01331 (M.D. Pa. July 12, 2009).
8. Indictment, *supra* note i, pp. 9, 18.
9. *Id.* p. 6–7.
10. Receiver's Initial Report at 5, 9, *Healy,* No. 09-cv-01331 (M.D. Pa. July 30, 2009).
11. *Id.* at 18–22.
12. *Id.* at 17.
13. *Id.* at 11–12.
14. *Id.* Inventory at 1–10.
15. *Id.* Inventory at 13–15.
16. Complaint, *supra* note vii, p. 34; Receiver's Third Report at 4, *Healy,* No. 09–01331 (M.D. Pa. Apr. 15, 2010).
17. Indictment, *supra* note i, p. 8.
18. *Id.* p. 11.
19. *Id.* p. 12.
20. *Id.* p. 14.
21. *Id.* p. 15.
22. Press Release, U.S. Department of Justice, *Florida Man Indicted in $20 Million Ponzi Scheme That Targeted Pennsylvania Investors,* October 15, 2009.
23. Arrest Warrant, attach. Report of Bail Violations, *Healy,* No. 09-cr-00319 (M.D. Pa. Dec.18, 2009).
24. *Healy,* No. 09-cr-00319 (M.D. Pa. Jan. 7, 2010) (Order).
25. *Healy,* No. 09-cr-00319 (M.D. Pa. Apr. 1, 2010) (Judgment in a Criminal Case).
26. Notice of Appeal to U.S. Court of Appeals, Third Circuit, *United States v. Healy,* No. 10–2095 (3rd Cir. Apr. 12, 2010).
27. *Healy,* No. 09-cv-01331 (M.D. Pa. June 22, 2010) (Consent Order of Permanent Injunction).
28. Memorandum and Order of Judge Christopher Connor, United Sates District Court for the Middle District of Pennsylvania, 1:09-CV-1331 (April 26, 2011).

CHAPTER TEN

1. Obituary, *Ryan Duane Puckett,* Charlotte Observer, June 24–25, 2009.
2. Appendix to Memorandum in Support of Plaintiff's Motion for a Statutory Restraining Order Ex. 3: Declaration p. 6, *CFTC v. Barki, LLC,* 09-cv-00106 (W.D. N.C. Mar. 17, 2009).

3. App. to Pl.'s Mem., *supra* note ii, at Ex. 1: Decl. pp. 8–10, 13.

4. *Id.* pp. 2–6, 10.

5. *Id.* pp. 13–15.

6. *Id.* pp. 17–23, Ex. 5: Decl. pp. 20–25.

7. App. to Pl.'s Mem. *supra* note ii, Ex. 1: Decl. p. 24.

8. Complaint for Injunctive Relief, Civil Monetary Penalties, and Other Equitable Relief, *CFTC v. Barki, LLC,* No. 09-cv-00106 (W.D. N.C. Mar. 17, 2009); Barki, LLC, No. 09-cv-00106 (W.D. N.C. Mar. 17, 2009) (Order Granting Plaintiff's Motion for Statutory Restraining Order).

9. Complaint, *supra* note viii, pp. 1, 23–28.

10. *Id.*, pp. 33–37, 40–41.

11. Answer of Relief Defendant Rhonda Kramer, *Barki, LLC,* No. 09-cv-00106 (W.D. N.C. May 6, 2009); App. to Pl.'s Mem. *supra* note ii, Ex. 1: Decl. p.16, Ex. 3: Decl. p.15.

12. App. to Pl.'s Mem. *supra* note ii, Ex. 3: Decl. pp. 3–13.

13. App. to Pl.'s Mem. *supra* note ii, Ex. 2: Decl. pp. 4–6.

14. *Id.* pp. 8–9.

15. Receiver's First Report at 7–8, *Barki, LLC,* No. 09–00106 (W.D. N.C. May 18, 2009).

16. Barki, LLC Receivership Information, http://www.gnerlaw.com/Barki.

17. Receiver's Motion for Approval of Settlement pp. 11–15, *Barki, LLC,* No. 09-cv-00106 (W.D. N.C. May 10, 2010).

INVESTORS' BILL OF RIGHTS

1. *The Investors' Bill of Rights* is reprinted with permission from the National Futures Association. All rights reserved.

About The Author

Bart Chilton has more than twenty-five years of government experience. His career includes service in the US House of Representatives, the US Senate, the Executive Branch, and at two independent agencies. In 2007, he was nominated to the CFTC by President Bush and confirmed by the US Senate. In 2009, he was nominated again by President Obama and reconfirmed. During his service at the CFTC, Commissioner Chilton has been an advocate for consumers and businesses alike. In 2008, he began calling for financial reform of unregulated "dark markets" and limits on excessive speculation, including traders he calls "massive passives." Since 2010, he has sought greater accountability and oversight of high-frequency traders, whom he has termed "cheetah traders" due to their exceptional speed. He is a frequently quoted opinion leader, who appears regularly on financial and business television programs in the United States and abroad.

He can be reached at bchilton@cftc.gov.